Towards Shockproof European Legal and Governance Strategies

Stavros Zouridis, Sam Muller
and Peter Polakovic (editors)

2018
Torkel Opsahl Academic EPublisher
Brussels

EDITORS' PREFACE

For decades, the rule of law as defined by the Venice Commission has been a success formula for Europe's prosperity, development, and happiness. Given past experiences in and outside Europe, we know that the rule of law can never be taken for granted. This self-constraining mode of government requires continuous political and public support. It also requires strong governments that can deal with checks and balances. The past few years, the rule of law in Europe has been increasingly challenged. Migration, radicalisation, terrorism but also unemployment, inequality, and the stability of the Euro have all required rapid and effective policy responses. Too many constraints on governments are then easily considered as threats to the effectiveness of policies. This may explain the decline in the political and public support for the rule of law throughout Europe.

Obviously, getting rid of the rule of law and the *Rechtsstaat* would be tantamount to throwing away the baby with the bathwater. This may even threaten the very sources of Europe's wealth, development, and legitimacy. The rule of law guarantees reliable and non-corrupt governments that promote social trust and inclusive societies. An erosion of the rule of law may thus result in less social trust and social capital in Europe. On the other side, simply reiterating the principles underlying the rule of law and imposing sanctions on those governments that do not comply with these principles will also not generate and sustain the necessary political and public support for the rule of law. As German legal theorists have convincingly argued at the end of the nineteenth century: the rule of law should contribute to achieving social goals and political purposes in order to become sustainable and legitimate.

In Europe reinventing the rule of law and adapting it to contemporary society thus requires a thorough reflection on the very foundations and shape of the *Rechtsstaat*. This volume aims to contribute to this process by bringing together experiences from different legal and political-science perspectives and various parts of the world. We hope that those who deeply care about the rule of law as a European foundation will benefit from these experiences in order to build a rule of law that will truly guide Europe during the coming decades.

i

We are grateful to the contributors. As an editorial team we really tested their patience and generosity, and we are proud that we are all finally rewarded with this book. We are also grateful to the European Commission for funding the FLAGSHIP research project that triggered this volume.

Stavros Zouridis
Professor of Public Administration, Tilburg University

Sam Muller
Director, HiiL

Peter Polakovic
Research Assistant, HiiL

TABLE OF CONTENTS

1

The Future of Law and the Law of the Future

Stavros Zouridis, Sam Muller and Peter Polakovic*

In 2011, we published the world's first *Law of the Future Scenarios*.[1] It was an attempt to picture the trends most relevant for the global legal environment towards 2030. For those who do not know: scenarios are neither predictions on what the future will look like nor images of desirable futures. Quite the contrary: they are wind tunnels in which strategies can be tested for robustness, in a variety of winds.

By publishing these scenarios, we hoped to provoke more future-oriented thinking about legal systems. Rather than moving along law-by-law, court-case by court-case, election-by-election, we hoped we could stimulate a longer, more strategic approach to how we might want our legal systems to change.

At the time of publication of the scenarios, at least two beliefs seemed persistent. Despite the economic and financial crises triggered by the bankruptcy of Lehman Brothers in 2007 and the many crises that Europe has encountered since, the debate on the European Union ('EU') was first guided by a belief in multilateral and supranational legal and governance regimes. Even at the time of writing in 2018, this belief seems unshakeable. For example, the European Commission in 2017 published a white paper on the future of Europe. Whereas our scenarios have been developed in order to prepare for an uncertain global legal environment, the European Commission presented five scenarios as policy options. These policy options are presented as neutral, but the descriptions of the scenarios implicitly assume that European solutions for problems are better than national

* **Stavros Zouridis** is Professor of Public Administration at the Tilburg School of Governance (Tilburg University). **Sam Muller** is Director of The Hague Institute for the Internationalisation of Law ('HiiL'). **Peter Polakovic** is Research Assistant at HiiL.
1. Sam Muller *et al.* (eds.), *The Law of the Future and the Future of Law*, Torkel Opsahl Academic EPublisher ('TOAEP'), Oslo, 2011.

ones. For example, in describing the pros and cons of the scenario 'Those who want more do more', the European Commission argues that the gap between public expectations and actual governance performance starts to close in the countries that want and choose to do more. Hence, the assumption is that European solutions are intrinsically more effective than national solutions. When our scenarios were published, there was a widespread idea that globalisation creates new transnational problems that, in turn, require legal and governance solutions that transcend national boundaries. Even in 2018, politicians who question the inevitability of such a progression are usually referred to as populists. The banking and fiscal crises spurred a second belief at the start of this decade – next to the necessity of international governance and law, these crises allegedly proved that private legal and governance mechanisms of self-regulation do not work. Self-regulation and private governance regimes were increasingly questioned, fuelled by financial crises and industrial scandals (such as the emissions scandal in the EU). In turn, we observed a strong demand for international public governance regimes.

Our scenarios opened up alternative futures for the global legal and governance environment. Some seven years after we first published the *Law of the Future Scenarios*, we have decided to produce an update herein. We seek here to answer the questions: Which scenarios seem to evolve? What trends can be observed in the global legal and governance environment? A framework for such an update has been provided by the EU-funded FLAGSHIP project. Using the European Commission's White Paper as a point of departure, we have been able to re-think both the trends and the scenarios, and use the scenarios as a wind tunnel to test the robustness of the legal and governance strategies of the European Commission. The chapters in this volume reflect on the trends that underlie the *Law of the Future Scenarios*, and serve as a third building block for testing the robustness of the EU's legal and governance strategies.

In this introduction, we summarize the subsequent chapters and use insights borne thereof to conduct such testing. This chapter starts with a brief explanation of the *Law of the Future Scenarios* and a recapitulation of the EU's legal and governance strategies (section 1.1). Next, we briefly summarize the key insights of the papers (section 1.2). Finally, we explore the implications of testing the robustness of the EU's legal and governance strategies (section 1.3).

1.1. The Law of the Future Scenarios and the EU's Legal and Governance Strategies

1.1.1. The Law of the Future Scenarios

Scenarios are used in contexts in which uncertainty is ubiquitous. The *Law of the Future Scenarios* focus on the global legal and governance environment in which authoritative rule-making, rule-enforcement, and processes of dispute resolution take place. Conceptually, the global legal environment does not imply that rules are made that span the entire globe or that these rules are globally enforced. In our definition, the global legal environment refers to a multi-layered phenomenon including all mechanisms of authoritative rule-making, rule-enforcement, and dispute resolution that transcend national borders. It emerges out of the actions of both public and private legal actors, the ideas and research of legal scholars, and the initiatives and actions of international institutions. Even though national legislators' behaviour affects the global legal and governance environment, it emerges to a large extent without being directed. There is no Chief Executive Officer. Basically, we therefore assume that the future of the global legal and governance environment is uncertain. We need scenarios to deal with the future uncertainties.

The research that led to the *Law of the Future Scenarios* started with mapping major trends in the global legal and governance environment. The outcomes were published in two extensive volumes that include contributions from a substantial number of legal scholars and lawyers from different disciplines and different parts of the world.[2]

From these papers and a number of workshops we held in different parts of the world, we distilled two major trends – the internationalisation of law and the growth of private governance regimes. These trends are not new and have extensively been mapped elsewhere.[3] Both will be briefly explained hereinafter.

---

[2]   *Ibid.* And Sam Muller, Stavros Zouridis, Morly Frishman and Laura Kistemaker (eds.): *The Law of the Future and the Future of Law: Volume II*, TOAEP, The Hague, 2012.

[3]   For example, Jan Klabbers and Mortimer Sellers (eds.), *The Internationalization of Law and Legal Education*, Springer, London, 2009; Michael Joachim Bonell, "The CISG, European Contract Law and the Development of a World Contract Law", in *American Journal of Comparative Law*, 2008, vol. 56, no. 1, p. 3 on law beyond the state.

First, a growing patchwork of international law, international institutions, and transnational co-operation is observed. Growing international trade has gone along with the internationalisation of contract law, torts, business law, and intellectual property law. Since national laws are not harmonised, conflicts and gaps between national laws are increasingly revealed. These conflicts exert pressure on governments to harmonise their legislation and their legal systems. The internationalisation of law thus refers to growing interdependencies and interchange between national legal systems and the accommodation of national legal systems to these interdependencies and interchange. Internationalisation is a global trend but it is not happening in the same way, with the same depth, and in the same areas across the world. Two important clarifications must be made. First, legal globalisation and the rise of global governance do not mean that a coherent corpus of law is evolving that spans the whole globe. Legal globalisation and the globalisation of governance refer to a patchwork both with regard to the legal and governance areas involved and to the extent of internationalisation. For example, the legal globalisation of trade law mainly occurs on the regional level. The EU is probably the most far-reaching instance. Different legal areas also seem to evolve at a different pace. For example, the internationalisation of trade law seems to move faster than the internationalisation of criminal procedure. The internationalisation of law and governance neither implies voluntarism nor a consciously-built body of global law. Instead, incidents, crises, and the continuous manifestation of new problems are the primary drivers of the process.

The growth of private governance regimes for rule-making, rule-enforcement, and dispute resolution indicate a second major trend. Both national and international law have, for many years, firmly rested on public authority and state institutions. Nevertheless, new private regimes seem to be booming. These private regimes appear in different shapes. A business sector, sometimes together with non-governmental organisations ('NGOs'), can set standards, guidelines, or rules concerning governance or liabilities. For example, the Brewers of Europe have enacted the *Responsible Commercial Communications Guidelines for the Brewing Industry*.[4] The timber industry – with the Forest Stewardship Council – produced

---

[4] The Brewers of Europe, *Responsible Commercial Communications: Guidelines for the Brewing Industry*, 2012.

standards on sustainable logging and the sale of timber.[5] Sometimes an industry creates a standard contract or agreement. The Model Mine Development Agreement, developed in consultation with mining companies, governments, and civil society within the context of the International Bar Association, is a prime example.[6] Another facet of this trend is the growing use of alternative dispute resolution mechanisms instead of court systems. The eBay/PayPal resolution centre solves around 60 million disagreements between buyers and sellers every year. In the EU, a Common Frame of Reference for European Private Law was drafted and freely made available on the Internet.[7] This was not a government initiative; instead it sprang forth from European legal scholars. It has now become a point of reference for legislators and courts in the EU.

The trend towards privatisation of law also requires some elaboration to prevent misunderstanding. First, the rise of private regimes does not mean that these are isolated from legal regimes created by public authorities. For example, private initiatives may spark off public regulation. Secondly, here too, we see wide diversity. Private regimes may refer to rules, standards or guidelines but may also refer to authoritative mechanisms of dispute resolution. The term 'soft law' may be used, but in their actual effect, guidelines can sometimes be as 'hard' as law. Whereas a large-scale business organisation may not be touched by an administrative fine of several million Euros, it may fear not having access to a stock exchange due to non-compliance with the code of conduct regarding child labour.

There is no reason to assume that these trends will continue in the same direction and at the same pace. Moreover, there are several clues that they may also reverse. For example, both within the EU and in other parts of the world, national borders, national identity, and national interests are being re-discovered. The Brexit referendum and its aftermath, the growth of nationalist political parties in many European countries, the election of president Trump and his agenda of putting America first, and the growing self-consciousness of the Russian state indicate that national borders have

---

5   Forest Stewardship Council, *Forest Management Standards*, 2010.

6   Mining Law Committee of the International Bar Association, *Model Mining Development Agreement Project*, available on the project web site, last accessed 9 March 2017.

7   Study Group on a European Civil Code and the Research Group on EC Private Law, *Principles, Definitions and Model Rules of European Private Law: Draft Common Frame of Reference*.

not become obsolete. Both the internationalisation and the privatisation of law and governance should therefore be regarded as uncertainties or contingencies for the future global legal and governance environment. Will we witness continued internationalisation of rules and institutions or will this trend reverse? Both futures are possible. International trade, communication, travel, migration, and such phenomena that transcend national borders will generate international interdependencies that in turn require law and governance. Simultaneously, we observe a renaissance of national interest and national borders. Whether internationalisation of law and governance will continue in the next decades remains to be seen. The same applies to the privatisation of law and governance. Will private governance mechanisms and private legal regimes further expand and become dominant, or will state-connected institutions and legal regimes retain their position? Currently, there is no decisive trend that indicates either one of these futures. Instead, both futures can already be observed in their embryonic stages. If the two trends are regarded as uncertainties or contingencies, they point at four possible future scenarios.

Taken together, these contingencies conceptually allow four different scenarios (see Table 1 below).

	Growth of private governance regimes	Reversed growth private governance regimes
Internationalisation of law	Legal Internet	Global Constitution
Reversed internationalisation of law	Legal Tribes	Legal Borders

Table 1. Global legal and governance scenarios.

These scenarios picture possible global legal and governance environments that may emerge in the next decades.[8] Regarding the names we have given each of the scenarios, rather than taking them for their literal meaning, one ought to bear in mind that they refer to metaphors meant to convey the central feature of each scenario. Thus, 'Global Constitution' does not imply there will actually be a single world constitution, but rather, that in this scenario the global legal environment will increasingly resemble an international constitutional order. In 'Legal Internet', the name does not mean that this scenario is about the Internet. Instead, it implies that the global legal environment in this world is characterised by a decentralized transnational network involving a big range of actors in which co-ordination, governance, rule-making and so on are not regulated from the top. Similarly, 'Legal Tribes' does not denote a world that is composed of tribes, rather, it hints to a reality whereby the global legal environment is composed of many relatively small 'communities' with relatively little contact and co-ordination, and a weaker role for the state. Finally, 'Legal Borders' does not imply that legal walls will be built between national legal systems, but instead emphasises the increased importance or renaissance of national and regional sovereignty.

These scenarios reveal quite different possible futures for 2030. In the 'Global Constitution' scenario, an international constitutional order would have emerged during the next decades, slowly but surely covering all major legal areas on a global scale – trade, environment, security, crime, finance, markets and competition, intellectual property, labour, taxation, and health – leaving only a few areas untouched by international rules and procedures. Global law would not be driven by a specific set of values or leading legal systems. Instead, the process of blending would, to a large extent, be eclectic. Whereas global competition law and contract law would be primarily fuelled by free market ideals, global criminal law would be led by retaliatory principles. It would therefore become more punitive and strict than European countries are used to. The principle of legality – all governments are bound by law – would be the broadly accepted principle underlying the global legal environment. The global constitutional order would not be based on one document or charter, but rather on a series of charters and constitution-like documents, in which international regulators,

---

[8] See also Sam Muller *et al.*, *Law Scenarios to 2030*, HiiL, 2012.

adjudicators, and courts would be defined and connected with each other. This multi-layered system would be complex, and at times Byzantine. The rules and institutions that make up this global legal environment would be difficult to change once formalised. The enforcement of rules would be public in nature, or a clear derivative thereof.

In the 'Legal Borders' scenario, national and regional legislation would become the primary source of rule-making in 2030. Regional and sub-regional organisations would be the ultimate defence against what would widely be perceived as out-of-control international institutions and an international environment in which common values would be scarce. The international level would be for politics, not law. There would be a lot less talk about universality than there once was. In fact, most would agree that there is no universality. With regional legal pluralism, the rule of law would also be regionally pluralised. As a consequence, context-specific regional and national interpretations of concepts such as fundamental human rights, separation of church and state, balance of powers, and the principle of legality would prevail. The international institutions that were developed at the end of the twentieth century would slowly erode and lose their significance. In some instances, states would withdraw ratifications, in others they would be being minimally interpreted at best, and otherwise completely ignored. International courts – insofar as they are given adequate funding – would face strong pressure to reduce their footprint and the scope of their decisions. Enforcement would also be a national affair. In some areas, such as environmental law, enforcement would be loosely co-ordinated on a regional level to prevent natural disasters.

In the 'Legal Internet' scenario, rules – in the sense that lawyers are used to – would be a lot less important in 2030. New generations would have become acquainted with new ways of rule-making, law enforcement, and resolving disputes. Reputation, trust, transparency, mobilisation of voice, and demonstrated effectiveness would be the new mechanisms to secure a social and political order. Formal rules and procedures would be considered old-fashioned, too formal, ineffective, too uniform, and too inflexible. Public rules would gradually be replaced or marginalised by standards developed by private actors. Monitoring and even enforcement would be dealt with by private regimes and mechanisms created by the parties involved. Democracy or accountability would be less a matter of working through parliaments and more a matter of working through interest groups and loosely organised structures that operate between interest groups. Self-regulation would be the prime source of legitimacy. Private rule-making, enforcement, and dispute resolution mechanisms would usually be flexible and efficient, whereas public regimes would be more bureaucratic and rigid. The absence of clear, all-encompassing organising principles, like the principle of legality, the United Nations ('UN') definition of the rule of law, or state sovereignty, would make the global legal environment complex, often confusing and largely unstable.

Finally, in the 'Legal Tribes' scenario, the global legal environment would witness a severe loss of relevance of the state combined with a loss of interest in internationalisation. In this scenario, by 2030, the global legal environment would consist of a largely unconnected group of communities that govern themselves. In many ways states would become failed states. Global security would be a serious issue and law would have been completely abandoned as a way to achieve it. Local security, which would be mainly self-organised, would be the main basis for ordering. Besides, order would be local and mainly privatised, maintained through a small-scale networks of security corporations, communities and civil society organisations, and supported, where possible and useful, by small public structures. The state and the international global legal environment would wither away. International organisations would lose their relevance and close due to lack of interest, funds, effectiveness, and legitimacy. Next to state borders, the global legal environment would also witness religious borders, borders organised around economic activities, ethnic borders, and political borders. The old regional organisations would lose much of their economic *raison d'être*. The successful ones would transform into security alliances: public-private regional fences within which smaller communities could conduct economic activity on a larger than local scale. The main role of the public realm would be to deal with the link between the huge variety of private, self-regulatory regimes. But with a greatly reduced tax base, resources would be limited. As a leading principle, the rule of law would have become an anachronistic concept. Enforcement would be a local and mostly private affair. Social control, groups taking justice into their own hands, and militias maintaining order would be predominant in many parts of the world, whereas religious or public authorities would take up these tasks in other regions.

1.1.2. The EU's Legal and Governance Strategies

As indicated above, these scenarios were first presented in 2011 as a means to provoke a future-oriented debate on law and governance built on uncertainty and analysis instead of ideology and policy. One would expect public institutions to adopt a learning behaviour that accords with the adage, once bitten, twice shy. Thus, we would anticipate that the European debate on the future of law and governance would have become more open for the scenarios after a series of events that shook previously unshakeable beliefs. The migration crisis, the continuing Euro crisis, Brexit and more generally the dramatically declining political support for international, multilateral, and supranational institutions compels European institutions to get involved in some serious double-loop learning.[9] Double-loop learning requires questioning fundamental assumptions in order to align them with the societal and political environment. Is it truly natural for law and governance to increasingly shift towards transnational institutions? Is the internationalisation of law and governance necessarily a linear and inevitable historical process? Should governments not also take into account the possibility that this process could reverse, and be strategically prepared for that eventuality?

Double-loop learning is both difficult and rare in public organisations and institutions. The European Commission can hardly be seen as an exception in this respect. Its recently published 'White Paper on the Future of Europe' demonstrates the difficulty in questioning the very foundations on which it is built.[10] In its White Paper, the European Commission does question its role and position, but even the most minimal scenario imaginable by the European Commission – the 'Nothing but the single market' scenario – entails more European Union. The EU would then focus on 'deepening certain key aspects of the single market'. We would argue that major shifts in the global legal and governance environment, as depicted in our scenarios, require a fundamental re-thinking of these foundations and strategies. Instead of double-loop reflection in the realm of legal and governance

---

9   Chris Argyris, *On Organizational Learning*, Blackwell Publishers, Oxford, 1993.

10 European Commission, *White Paper on the Future of Europe: Reflections and scenarios for the EU27 by 2025*, COM (2017) 2025, 1 March 2017 (http://www.legal-tools.org/doc/b2888a/).

strategies, we observe that the European Commission does not move beyond single-loop learning and stricter enforcement of existing strategies.

For example, in March 2014, the European Commission decided to adopt a new, proactive rule of law policy. In its communication, the European Commission presented a new EU framework to strengthen the rule of law.[11] In its rule of law strategy presented by the European Commission in March 2015, the Commission concludes that the current EU legal framework is not adequate for addressing internal, systemic threats to the rule of law and more generally EU values. This conclusion is drawn after some rule of law-related crises. Former EU Justice Commissioner Reding mentioned some concrete examples of these crises in a speech given on 4 September 2013,[12] including the French government's attempt in 2010 to implement a collective deportation policy aimed at EU citizens of Romani ethnicity, the Hungarian government's attempt to implement an early mandatory retirement policy for the judiciary and the non-compliance of the Romanian government with judgments of the national constitutional court in 2012. The rule of law strategy emphasises that the EU legal framework is no longer adequate due to non-compliance by governments. Double-loop learning would imply a reflection on whether the legal framework still matches with the European social and political context and, if not, what changes should be implemented. Instead, the European Commission decides to focus only on a stricter enforcement of the framework, including penalties. It does not ask a number of questions, such as whether the thick approach of the rule of law[13] still builds on the social conventions and generalized morality in Europe, or whether this approach to the rule of law produces adverse and politically-undesirable effects. The same applies to the external legal strategy of the European Commission. With regard to its external policies and global legal strategies, Article 3(5) (previously Article

---

[11] European Commission Communication, *A New EU Framework to Strengthen the Rule of Law*, COM (2014) 158 Final, 11 March 2014 (http://www.legal-tools.org/doc/7f7703/).

[12] Dimitry Kochenov and Laurent Pech, *Upholding the Rule of Law in the EU: On the Commission's 'Pre-Article 7 Procedure' as a Timid Step in the Right Direction*, Robert Schuman Centre for Advanced Studies, Research Paper No. 2015/24, 2015.

[13] See Brian Z. Tamanaha, *On the Rule of Law: History, Politics, Theory*, Cambridge University Press, Cambridge, 2004.

2(5)) of the Treaty on European Union ('TEU') provides some strict guidelines. It stipulates:[14]

> In its relations with the wider world, the Union shall uphold and promote its values and interests and contribute to the protection of its citizens. It shall contribute to peace, security, the sustainable development of the Earth, solidarity and mutual respect among peoples, free and fair trade, eradication of poverty and the protection of human rights, in particular the rights of the child, as well as to the strict observance and the development of international law, including respect for the principles of the United Nations Charter.

The external rule of law approach includes both formal and substantive versions and it appears as thick as the internal rule of law approach (see, for instance, Articles 21 and 23 of the TEU). The same principles should be taken into account in the relations between the EU and its neighbours (see Article 8 of the TEU). Second, with regard to the global legal environment TEU also explicitly addresses the ideals to be strived for. Article 21(1) of the TEU reads:

> The Union's action on the international scene shall be guided by the principles which have inspired its own creation, development and enlargement, and which it seeks to advance in the wider world: democracy, the rule of law, the universality and indivisibility of human rights and fundamental freedoms, respect for human dignity, the principles of equality and solidarity, and respect for the principles of the United Nations Charter and international law.
>
> The Union shall seek to develop relations and build partnerships with third countries, and international, regional or global organisations which share the principles referred to in the first subparagraph. It shall promote multilateral solutions to common problems, in particular in the framework of the United Nations.

The framework of the UN appears to be the EU's most desired framework for multilateral co-operation. Global economic integration and global harmonisation of the rule of law and human rights are also explicitly stated in Article 21 of the TEU to be the goals of the external (including

---

[14] Treaty on European Union, 7 February 1992, 92/C 191/01 (http://www.legal-tools.org/doc/806147/).

international) policies of the EU. For example, the external policies should be directed towards promoting an international system based on stronger multilateral co-operation and good global governance, as set out in Article 21(2)(h) of the TEU. In its Stockholm programme, the European Council reaffirms the importance of promoting fundamental rights both within and outside the EU. The Council argues that the 'values of the Union should be promoted and strict compliance with and development of international law should be respected'.[15] The programme also defines the key partners of the EU, in particular:

- Candidate countries and countries with an EU membership perspective, for which the main objective would be to assist them in transposing the *acquis*;
- European neighbourhood countries, and other key partners with whom the EU should co-operate on all issues in the area of freedom, security and justice;
- European Economic Area/Schengen states which have a close relationship with the Union;
- The United States ('US'), the Russian Federation and other strategic partners with which the EU should co-operate on all issues in the area of freedom, security and justice;
- Other countries or regions of priority, in terms of their contribution to EU strategic or geographical priorities; and
- International organisations such as the UN and the Council of Europe with whom the EU needs to continue to work and within which the EU should co-ordinate its position.

With regard to international organisations, the Council reaffirms the UN as the foundation for global governance in its Stockholm programme:

> The UN remains the most important international organisation for the Union. The Lisbon Treaty creates the basis for more coherent and efficient Union participation in the work of the UN and other international organisations.
>
> The Union should continue to promote European and international standards and the ratification of international

---

[15] European Council, *The Stockholm Programme – An Open and Secure Europe Serving and Protecting Citizens*, 2010/C 115/01, 4 May 2010 (http://www.legal-tools.org/doc/c6ada7/).

conventions, in particular those developed under the auspices
of the UN and the Council of Europe.

Strengthening the UN is also a cornerstone of the European Security
and Defence Policy. The EU appears to prefer a multilateral global order in
which the UN is positioned at the top. In its policies, the European Council
also chooses to co-operate with regional organisations (such as the African
Union and the Association of Southeast Asian Nations) and global players
like the US and China.

In this recapitulation of the EU's legal and governance strategies, we
observe a strong reliance on the 'Global Constitution' scenario. The analysis of the rule of law strategies of the European Commission and the EU
clearly indicates that there is a European desire for a global constitution.
The strategies thus anticipate on a 'Global Constitution' scenario in which
multilateral public authorities dominate as the entities that create and uphold law and settle transnational disputes. These public authorities should
be governed by 'thicker' rule of law principles. Other scenarios are not included or taken into account in the legal strategies of the European Commission and the EU which makes them vulnerable to changes in the global
legal environment.

Second, it seems plausible that, if other scenarios occur, they will
severely impede the effectiveness and tenability of the current rule of law
strategy. Both movements along the axis (more privatisation and less internationalisation) will render these strategies void. In case of further privatisation, the rule of law strategy may actually still be pursued, but it would
be overtaken by private mechanisms that better regulate and enforce law,
and perhaps even the rule of law. Whether rule of law principles are included in private legal and governance mechanisms does not seem to matter
because the legal strategies of the European Commission only aim at public
authorities, hence the 'Global Constitution' scenario. In case of reversed
internationalisation, the legal strategy would anticipate only a limited extent of grassroots rule of law development.

Third, the existing legal strategies do not seem very flexible in the
sense that it is possible to switch to alternative strategies in case other scenarios evolve. Because of the narrow focus on 'Global Constitution' and
the inflexibility of that scenario, the lead time for any other scenario may
be quite long. Whereas the rule of law strategy of the European

Commission and the EU seems to be evidence-based, it hardly appears to be future-proof.

1.2. The Global Legal and Governance Environment: Trends and Uncertainties

1.2.1. Ambiguity and Uncertainty are Here to Stay

This volume reflects on the robustness of the European legal and governance strategies as sketched above. It aims at capturing some of the major trends and hiccups in the global legal and governance environment, and it thus provides building blocks for future-proof legal and governance strategies. With the scenarios in mind, we asked a number of great minds to reflect on topical developments and the future of law and governance. The papers in this volume point towards a growing ambiguity and uncertainty of the global legal environment.

The demolition of the Berlin wall in 1989 heralded a new era and infused the world with the promise of a new world order. Politics would transform into regulatory governance, political controversies would transform into management issues, global markets would accelerate the wealth of nations, and if borders would not dissolve completely, they would at least become permeable. The ideology of globalisation and the spirit of cosmopolitanism seized the world and became the roadmaps towards global prosperity, freedom, and welfare.

Globalisation also affected the global legal and governance environment. In general, because of globalisation, the rule of law would become one of the cornerstones of governments all over the world. For a long time, many indications supported these hypotheses. Both the rule of law in its 'thin' meaning (that is, the principle of lawfulness or legality) and in its 'thick' meaning (including democracy and fundamental rights) spread across the globe. For example, for many years, Freedom House demonstrated a global tendency towards freedom and the world witnessed a significant improvement in economic growth.

In 2007, the first cracks were observed in this ongoing process. The adoption of democracy, freedom, and rule of law in the world stagnated according to some indicators. But there were more signals that the promise of 1989 would not be fulfilled, at least not in the short-run. First, the dark sides of globalisation increasingly revealed themselves and dominated the public and political agenda. Globalisation goes along with increasing prosperity and increased living standards, but also with dramatic growth of transnational crime, illicit trade, terrorism, global inequality, and uncontrolled migration. Second, the financial and economic crises triggered in 2008 demonstrated that global interdependencies could also cause major economic damage. Third, a new geo-political power balance seemed to evolve partly because of the economic rise of some countries and the simultaneous economic stagnation in the Western world. Naim observes a major power shift from previously strong formal institutions such as governments, international organisations, and global corporations, to the grassroots level and small-business entrepreneurs.[16] Kagan has observed a power shift from the US and Europe to a more balanced global constellation.[17] Whereas Europe was forced to focus on its internal crises, new global powers such as China and Russia entered the global law and governance arena.

The self-evident and sometimes even complacent belief in a global diffusion of the rule of law as interpreted by the EU has become inappropriate and unproductive. Contrary to some expectations, the world does not automatically appear to move towards Western interpretations of the rule of law. The self-evidence of a global linear historical process towards modernity as experienced in Europe is fundamentally contested by Comaroff and Comaroff.[18] Their argument is as follows:

> Contrary to the received Euromodernist narrative of the past two centuries – which has the global south tracking behind the curve of Universal History, always in deficit, always playing catch-up – there is good reason to think the opposite: that, given the unpredictable, under-determined dialectic of capitalism-and-modernity in the here and now, it is the south that often is the first to feel the effects of world-historical forces, the south in which radically new assemblages of capital and labor are taking shape, thus to prefigure the future of the global north.

---

[16] Moises Naim, *The End of Power: From Boardrooms to Battlefields and Churches to States, Why Being In Charge Isn't What It Used to Be*, Basic Books, New York, 2013.

[17] Robert Kagan, *The Return of History and the End of Dreams*, Alfred A. Knopf, New York, 2008.

[18] Jean Comaroff and John L. Comaroff, *Theory From the South: Or, How Euro-America is Evolving Toward Africa*, Routledge, London, 2012, p. 12.

Instead of a diffusion of belief systems and legal and governance institutions from Europe to the rest of the world, we may well witness the opposite. For example, the adverse effects of extreme neo-liberalism first emerged in Africa, Asia and Latin America in the 1990s, and the financial and economic crises in Europe and the US followed a decade later. Whereas other parts of the world have developed institutions to correct these effects, Europe is still in the process of developing these solutions. Comaroff and Comaroff argue that Europe has adopted some African belief systems to deal with these effects.[19] For example, African theories on participatory democracy, leadership, community, and accountability increasingly gain ground in Europe.

European and international institutions as well as national governments have developed responses to the crises that embody some of these major global changes. New transnational legal and governance institutions have been set up to cope with some of the dark sides of globalisation and some of the global economic and financial interdependencies. For example, treaties on cybercrime have been agreed upon, financial stability programmes have been erected, and new European instruments have been developed, such as the European arrest warrant. Existing global institutions have strengthened their positions and have been reformed to meet the demands of the new global balance of power. Last, but certainly not least, many private legal and governance mechanisms have evolved. Institutional adaptation has taken place not only on the transnational and international level. For example, a quest for new legal borders also reappeared as a response to the new global challenges.

Both the rapid succession of global crises and the urgent crisis response strategies demonstrate that the global legal environment has become both highly ambiguous and uncertain. The ambiguity arises from the many directions towards which these trends point at. Newly set up transnational and international legal institutions go along with new national legal borders, public attempts to respond to global challenges go along with rising private legal and governance mechanisms, and the rule of law both in its 'thin' meaning and in its 'thick' meaning has lost its self-evidence outside a small community of lawyers. The global legal environment has also become difficult to predict, with uncertainty characterising this environment

---

[19] *Ibid.*

due to the rapid pace of change. Economic, political, and social drivers of the global legal environment seem to change with ever-increasing pace – yesterday's coalitions may become tomorrow's enemies. Nobody can predict what the global legal and governance environment will look like in ten, twenty or thirty years. Of course, the community of lawyers may keep on believing in its scholastic rule of law interpretations and a predominantly public, multilateral, and supranational global legal environment. This belief system, however, will not be a sound basis for the strategies pursued by national and international law-makers in an increasingly ambiguous and uncertain global legal and governance environment. Thorough and continuous analysis and monitoring of the global legal and governance environment seems to be the only viable alternative to predictions and ideologies.

1.2.2. Shockproof Law and Governance in a Volatile World Order: Some Building Blocks

The chapters in this volume offer some building blocks for an assessment of the global legal and governance environment. As Joerges argues, transnational governance has too long been regarded as a technical matter. Instead of an emphasis on the regulation of global trade, he suggests a focus on the legitimacy of transnational governance. Borrowing from Karl Polanyi who stressed the social, cultural, and political embeddedness of trade and markets, Joerges argues that this basic notion may have been overlooked in previous trade agreements such as the General Agreement on Tariffs and Trade and those of the World Trade Organization. If the opposition and protests against the Transatlantic Trade and Investment Partnership ('TTIP') and the EU-Canada Comprehensive Economic and Trade Agreement ('CETA') are again neglected, the legitimacy impasse will continue and worsen. For a way out, Joerges reverts to a framework suggested by Rodrik. The globalisation trilemma hypothesis argues that it is impossible to simultaneously pursue trade globalisation, national autonomy, and democracy. Pursuing trade globalisation and national autonomy requires national governments to become technocratic and hence it will come at the cost of democracy. More democracy and trade globalisation require that transnational democratic legal and governance regimes are developed and that means that national autonomy has to be given up. Finally, combining national autonomy and democracy will negatively affect the level of trade globalisation. After an extensive analysis of the TTIP process, Joerges concludes that, given the current context, it would be wise to choose democracy and more national autonomy. Joerges accepts the limitations on further expansion of trade globalisation inherently connected with choosing for national autonomy and democracy.

In their paper, Renda and Cafaggi focus on transnational private regulation ('TPR'). They demonstrate the enormous variety of TPR schemes that have evolved during the past decades. TPR schemes nowadays include the involvement of private actors in the agenda-setting phase of policymakers, often alongside the implementation and enforcement of private rules. TPR schemes may also involve private transnational standards that complement public regulation. These schemes may be governed by experts, firms, NGOs or epistemic communities and global governance increasingly depends on TPR in order to meet the global challenges. Whereas TPR schemes are considered highly legitimate by the private actors involved, Renda and Cafaggi emphasise that they still experience a number of problems and challenges in the 'delivery' phase of their rules. In particular, compliance-monitoring and -enforcement need to be strengthened in order to make TPR schemes work better. Connecting public regulation with the TPR schemes may be useful to both accommodate better compliance monitoring and enforcement and achieve a better alignment of private benefits and social goals. According to Renda and Cafaggi, the "key opportunity is fully integrating TPR in international regulatory co-operation schemes aimed at tackling the most important societal problems". Further integration of public and private regulatory schemes may also prevent lock-in effects and self-indulgence in the evaluation of private regulatory bodies.

As argued above, the global legal and governance environment both displays uncertainty with regard to its future and ambiguity with regard to its current state. Williams provides an assessment of the current state of global governance. Based on his analysis that order and justice are conceptually closely connected, he argues that the international order urgently needs more justice. Williams distinguishes three conditions for a just international order. First, a just international order requires peace. However important, peace is not enough to achieve justice. Both adequate representation of individual and collective interests and the creation of "genuine opportunities for the development of states, communities, and individuals" are necessary to transform negative peace into positive peace. The absence of representation and equal opportunities on the global scale will produce an international order that is inherently unstable because it will lack legitimacy. Williams calls upon the UN to address this multi-faceted challenge:

> It is the UN, through the Security Council, that has the primary responsibility for maintaining international peace and security, and in so doing, preventing the eruption of deadly conflict which undermines both order and justice. It is the UN, furthermore, that provides all states with a representative forum, and through its institutional machinery can ensure that their interests are taken into account. *And it is the UN*, finally, which provides normative leadership, by advancing aims such as human rights, gender equality and sustainable development, through the work of its agencies, funds and programs, the policies agreed on by its members, and the public pronouncements of its leaders.

In order to play its necessary role to achieve a just international order, the UN should further reform. Representation can be improved in the Security Council and in the judicial institutions. Creating opportunity, the third pillar of a just international order, requires more than the UN. It should also include states and non-state actors.

An analysis of the current global legal and governance environment and its future runs the risk of a Western bias. A number of papers therefore focus on the global legal and governance environment from a non-Western perspective. The need for such a perspective is very much underscored by Mishina's paper on the Russian legal environment. Her analysis of legislative development in Russia clearly demonstrates that the Russian government is moving away from the principles and the global legal environment envisioned by Western governments. The government openly defies rulings of the European Court of Human Rights and increasingly criminalises the undesired use of political freedoms. According to Mishina, these legislative developments indicate further escalation of authoritarianism in Russia and even possible transformation into totalitarianism. These developments will dramatically affect the global legal and governance environment. Contrary to the just international order as portrayed by Williams with peace as a cornerstone, according to Mishina, Russia may be preparing for 'Cold War II'.

Russia's direct move away from the global legal environment, as envisioned by Europe and the US, and sketched by Mishina, points at erosion of the very foundations. With his analysis of the constitutionalisation process in Brazil, Neves indicates an opposite trend though it should be interpreted cautiously. On the surface, the gradual constitutionalisation of Brazil and its connectivity with the predominantly Inter-American legal institutions can be interpreted as a move towards global constitutionalism. Looking at the constitution and court decisions does not suffice to truly understand what is happening in Brazil. Underneath the legal and constitutional developments, Neves observes "a flaw in our capacity to implement liberal values". Obviously, the gradual constitutionalisation of Brazil should be understood as a long-term development that took place during the twentieth century. It would be too simplistic to interpret this process as the gradual adoption of Western constitutional conceptions by Brazil. Neves argues that a trans-constitutionalism would be a more appropriate concept to understand what happened:

> Trans-constitutionalism means that two or more legal orders or organisations, whether of the same kind or different kinds, engage simultaneously in the same constitutional case or problem.

Instead of the one-sided adoption of Inter-American and hence Western legal and governance conceptions, an interplay of legal conceptions is taking place. The relationship between the Inter-American human rights system, as introduced by the American Convention on Human Rights, and national Brazilian law provides an example of trans-constitutionalism. Neves mentions some cases in which the Brazilian constitution collides with the Inter-American legal regime. He concludes that the concept of trans-constitutionalism "offers a higher potential for effective constitutionalisation of several legal orders under different cultural contexts than models of cosmopolitan constitutionalism of Eurocentric or Western-centric base, which are not able to learn from the other".

In his paper, Ginsburg mentions Brazil as an example of constitutional flexibility. The constitution provided mandatory review after a trial period in order to test its workability. In a referendum five years after the adoption of the constitution, the Brazilian people decided on whether to retain presidentialism or adopt parliamentarism. Even though the voters decided to maintain presidentialism, this is clearly an example of constitutional flexibility. With an ever more volatile global legal environment, legal and governance orders urgently need flexible regimes. Ginsburg suggests at least three existing mechanisms of constitutional adjustment. First, constitutions can be amended. If amendment is allowed, constitutions usually include specific procedures and requirement for constitutional amendment.

A second mechanism for constitutional adjustment is interpretation. Ginsburg observes a global rise of constitutional review and supreme courts around the world "exercising powers that would have been unthinkable just a few decades ago". Constitutions can also be replaced. As Ginsburg argues "most constitutions die at a relatively young age". These mechanisms for constitutional adjustment provide some clues for a global legal environment that has to deal with increased volatility. Ginsburg therefore suggests an iterative global legal environment. Transitional, interim, or temporary deals for problems of international co-operation that have been broken down into "discrete component parts" may be useful solutions for the current impasse. The rigidity of treaty regimes may be softened with mandatory reviews such as the Brazilian referendum. Mandatory reviews oblige the states and other parties to renew their commitment and to bargain again for a better deal. Paradoxically, these flexibility mechanisms may provide for some stability of the global legal environment in a volatile world.

After these country perspectives from Russia and Brazil, the volume concludes with three papers that focus on specific substantive legal and governance challenges. In his contribution on transnational and international crime, Reichel addresses some trends and challenges in the global legal environment concerning these crimes. Whereas international crime refers to "acts that threaten the world order and security", the concept of transnational crime is used "for crimes that affect the interests of more than one state and are committed for personal gain and profit". The most common transnational crimes are the provision of illicit goods or service and the infiltration of business or government. Reichel's assessment of the current institutions to deal with these crimes is mixed. The International Criminal Court ('ICC') suggests that "there is considerable room for improvement". Instead of a global move away from the ICC, according to Reichel, it is more likely that the ICC will undergo some reforms – "especially in terms of having clearer and more realistic goals". With regard to transnational crime, Reichel sketches a more positive picture. He demonstrates that a variety of international instruments including bilateral and multilateral agreements have been set up to effectively deal with transnational crime:

> Problems do remain, however, and they are not insignificant.
> Issues or sovereignty are often raised, the ability (financial,
> technical, political and so on) of some countries to abide by
> agreements is difficult, human rights and privacy issues can

be challenging to reconcile, and competition among agencies/organisations presents barriers.

Reichel illustrates these challenges and problems with the example of human trafficking. What about the future of strategies to combat transnational crime? Reichel observes three developments. First, emerging crimes such as wildlife and forest crime as well as cybercrime will draw attention. Second, the gender bias will be corrected. More attention will be paid to women both as offenders and victims. Third, civil society and business will be included to a greater degree in strategies to combat transnational crimes:

> The role of governments and supra-national organisations is not expected to diminish, but we are likely to see an increased role for non-governmental organisations ('NGOs'), non-profit groups, and private companies (for example, ships increasingly use private security forces as they travel through areas at high risk for sea piracy).

Brammertz and Hughes paint an optimistic picture of international crime based on their experiences:

> Over these last two decades, international criminal justice has shown that it can achieve important results in practice. Hundreds of individuals have been tried and convicted for war crimes, crimes against humanity and genocide, including 80 by the ICTY to-date and 62 by the International Criminal Tribunal for Rwanda. Those brought to trial include senior political leaders like Charles Taylor (President of Liberia), Jean Kambanda (Prime Minister of Rwanda), Hissène Habré (President of Chad), Nikola Šainović (Deputy Prime Minister of Yugoslavia), Radovan Karadžić (President of the *Republika Srpska*) and Nuon Chea (Prime Minister of Cambodia).

Yet, at the same time, Brammertz and Hughes observe an increasing resistance to accountability. They also acknowledge that repeated attempts to establish justice processes for the most serious current conflicts have failed. As well as in the past international justice has to face the "critical challenge of obtaining state co-operation".

The increased role of national courts should be regarded as an opportunity to improve global justice. The future may also benefit from some lessons drawn by these experienced practitioners. Brammertz and Hughes suggest three key lessons. First, "the willingness of affected states to co-operate with justice mechanisms must be seen as decisive to the success of accountability processes and a key factor to influence. In other words, international justice requires diplomatic influence and persuasion to succeed". Second, "strategic pragmatism is often a necessary tool in pursuing accountability. Comprehensive justice must remain the ultimate goal. But because what is achievable will vary over time, an incremental approach may often be required". Finally, "affected states are more likely to agree to co-operate with justice mechanisms when the full spectrum of diplomatic tools is engaged and justice is linked to other desirable outcomes". Taken together, it is uncertain whether the experience with international criminal law of the past decades marks the end of its beginning or the beginning of its end. As can be expected from practitioners, they conclude that the risk of ineffective justice is critical but manageable. If the room for improvement signalled by Reichel is effectively dealt with, we may well have witnessed the end of the beginning of international criminal law.

This volume concludes with a contribution that may provide a glimpse as to the future of the global legal environment. As climate change has rapidly become a global problem that affects all parts of the world, albeit in different ways, the sense of urgency that global solutions are necessary has grown. In his contribution, Lefeber shows that global legal and governance solutions are possible even despite the trends indicated in the previous papers in this volume. Even though the New Global Climate Constitution has yet to prove itself, and the new US presidency has to commit itself to its development, this global regime demonstrates some lessons and conditions for global legal and governance regimes. As Lefeber argues, a global problem must be felt in all parts of the world and the problem definition must be supported by experts and science. Lefeber demonstrates that the "deadlock could only be overcome after science demonstrated that the dangerous anthropogenic interference with the climate system could only be avoided if all countries would contribute to mitigation". Second, the process in which the global regime is developed has to be "inclusive in terms of participation in the efforts to mitigate climate change and, therefore, potentially more effective in achieving the objective". Third, the process should not only include states and public authorities but also business and NGOs. Lefeber concludes that the "New Global Climate Constitution may have created the momentum for the emerging public-private partnerships and private-sector initiatives that contribute to mitigation, adaptation and acceptance of climate change, including the mobilization of financial resources". Finally, the global regime has to be backed by national legal institutions:

> Since the beginning of this century, there has been a prolifer-
> ation of climate change related cases in courts around the
> world. Many of these cases have been initiated by civil soci-
> ety.

The combination of scientific evidence of the global problem, the inclusiveness of the regime, and the support system of business, NGOs and national courts may provide some clues for a future global legal and governance environment that works even in an uncertain and volatile world.

1.3. Conclusions and Implications for European Legal Strategies

The ambiguity and uncertainty in the global legal and governance environment may be unprecedented, at least in recent history, but these characteristics are here to stay. It has become dangerous to rely on a stable legal and
governance strategy in the volatile global legal and governance environment. Strategies that do not build in uncertainty will become obsolete in no
time, with any single strategy certain to fail. Legal and governance strategies have to be plural to survive the ambiguous context in which they are
implemented. As demonstrated, the legal strategies of the EU and the European Commission do not sufficiently address the demands of the current
global legal environment. The 'thick' conception of the rule of law included
in both the European treaties and the policies of the European Commission,
as well as the self-evident nature of multilateral public legal and governance regimes, shows that these strategies are built on the assumption that
the 'Global Constitution' scenario will evolve. It is thus possible that the
European legal and governance strategies lack the flexibility and plurality
necessary to survive a volatile and ambiguous global legal and governance
environment.

With the chapters in this volume, we have aimed at making sense of
the current global legal and governance environment. Even though the topics and the assessment of the current situation differ substantially, there are
some general observations and common threads. A first commonality in the
chapters is the acknowledgement that neither internationalisation nor public authority, the cornerstones of the 'Global Constitution' scenario, can be
relied upon. In our scenarios we presented internationalisation and privatisation of global legal and governance regimes as key uncertainties. Both
trends could further mature but also reverse. It appears that most of the

authors in this volume observe a tendency to re-discover and re-install national borders while privatisation of law and governance is stronger than ever before. A second commonality in the chapters is the acknowledgement that the only global legal and governance mechanisms that work are those that are perceived as both inclusive and just. The regimes that work should encourage participation and equity of interests. Third, the global legal and governance regimes that work have to connect public and private transnational regulatory schemes. Transnational and global governance will only be effective and legitimate if it is built on public-private partnerships that combine the strengths of public authorities (particularly enforcement) and business, NGOs and local communities (particularly legitimacy and embeddedness).

These lessons and observations suggest that only a new generation of European legal and governance strategies will survive the future global legal and governance environment. Such strategies should first build on a combination of selective internationalisation of law and governance. While the existing strategies build on the assumption that the global legal and governance environment will evolve according to the 'Global Constitution' scenario, a new generation of European legal strategies has to include both the 'Legal Borders' and 'Legal Internet' scenarios. Internationalisation of law and governance is only appropriate if the problem is transnational and all partners on all levels – both public and private – are strongly committed.

Second, commitment on the national level requires participation and equity instead of a naïve belief that the European or Western models are superior to the interests of other parts of the world. Only legal and governance institutions that are globally perceived as inclusive and just will be legitimate and effective. For example, transnational institutions that are not perceived as such cannot rely on compliance and backing by national courts.

Finally, European legal and governance strategies should build on public-private partnerships. Transnational private regimes have become mature and urgently need connectivity with public regimes. Business, NGOs, communities, and other private parties have demonstrated the ability to set standards and develop dispute resolution regimes that work. In order to sustain such transnational private regimes, and to utilise their strengths, they should be included in the European legal and governance strategies.

A European legal and governance strategy built upon these principles will prove to be robust and increase the probability of surviving different global legal and governance environments. Instead of assuming that the world will evolve to a 'Global Constitution' scenario, such a strategy also takes into account the possibilities that the global legal and governance environment evolves according to the 'Legal Borders' and 'Legal Internet' scenarios. As Joerges demonstrates in this volume by using Rodrik's globalisation trilemma, the suggested legal and governance strategy mixes a choice of both strengthening democracy and national autonomy. Assuming that this trilemma is inevitable, a choice of a new generation of European legal and governance strategies also means a choice of less globalisation. Whether the disadvantages of less globalisation outweigh the advantages of a better aligned European legal and governance strategy is a political matter that we gladly leave to those elected to make this choice.

2

From Trade Liberalisation to Transnational Governance

Christian Joerges*

The title of my chapter alludes to a major challenge. The development to which it refers seems irresistible. International trade is a global phenomenon. It requires an institutional framework, and generates governance arrangements. The functioning of these arrangements is not just a technical matter – we should be concerned about the legitimacy impasses of transnational governance. This has become a topic of outstanding topicality with respect to mega-regional trade agreements such as the Transatlantic Trade and Investment Partnership ('TTIP'), and its little brother the EU-Canada Comprehensive Economic and Trade Agreement ('CETA').

'Legitimacy', as Max Weber has taught us, is not to be conceptualised as a sociological given, but as a construct which, in the Habermasian parlance, derives from 'trustworthiness'. As such, we have to consider whether these arrangements 'deserve recognition'. In the past, the move towards such agreements seemed simply irresistible, and their enormous complexity a solid barrier against critical political evaluation. At the time of writing, however, the future of these agreements is highly uncertain. An important source of such uncertainty are legitimacy concerns. These concerns were articulated, for instance, at a mobilising event in Berlin on 10 October 2015 which attracted some 150,000 protesters from all over Germany;[1] before the Federal Constitutional Court in Karlsruhe by 68,016 individual complainants and a broad range of institutional actors, all

---

* **Christian Joerges** is Professor of Law and Society at the Hertie School of Governance and Co-Director of the Centre of European Law and Politics at the University of Bremen.

[1] *Tagesschau.de*, "Großproteste in Berlin: Massenhaft gegen TTIP" [Big protests in Berlin: Massive against TTIP], 10 October 2015.

complaints that were taken seriously by the Court;[2] and by two Walloon Provinces which prevented the Kingdom of Belgium for the time being from signing CETA[3] – a resistance which could only be overcome by a Joint Interpretative Declaration of the EU and Canada.[4]

Intense political controversies are certainly significant signals. But these signals need to be deciphered. Mega-regional trade agreements like TTIP and CETA are illustrations of exemplary and fundamental importance in the realm of transnational governance. In order to understand this importance and evaluate its controversial aspects, some re-constructive exercises and theoretical deliberations about the international trade system and its development are indispensable. This analysis will be performed in three steps hereinafter. First, I will outline its theoretical framework, based upon the works of Dani Rodrik and Karl Polanyi (section 2.1.). This framework will then orient the following re-construction, which will depart from the General Agreement on Tariffs and Trade ('GATT') (section 2.2.), and finally proceed to its replacement in 1994 by the World Trade Organization ('WTO') and, against this background, explain the move towards TTIP (section 2.3.).

2.1. Transnational Governance, Polanyi's Economic Sociology and Rodrik's Trilemma Thesis

International trade is a core dimension of globalisation and, accordingly, international trade law is a highly developed sub-section of international economic law. The pertinent literature is overwhelming. I cannot but simply assert that there are good reasons to resort to the two above-mentioned

---

[2] Bundesverfassungsgericht [German Federal Constitutional Court], Judgment of 13 October 2016, 2 BvR 1368/16, 13 October 2016.

[3] Paul Magnette, Political Scientist and the Prime Minister of the Walloon Region was, in 2011, Minister of Economics in Belgium. His comments on the instruction he received from the Finnish Commissioner Olli Rehn are worth remembering: "Wie kent Olli Rehn? Wie heeft ooit het gezicht van Olli Rehn gezien? Wie weet waar hij vandaan komt en wat hij heeft gedaan? Niemand. Terwijl hij zegt hoe wij onze economische politiek moeten voeren" [Who knows who Olli Rehn [Commissioner for Economic and Monetary Affairs] is? Who has seen Olli Rehn's face? Who knows where he comes from and what he's done? Nobody. Yet he tells us how we should conduct our economic policy], as cited in "Brussels v Brussels: Belgium and the EU clash over the budget", in *The European Citizen*, 13 January 2012.

[4] European Commission, *Joint Interpretative Instrument on the Comprehensive Economic and Trade Agreement (CETA) between Canada and the European Union and its Member States*, OJEU L 11, 14 January 2017 (http://www.legal-tools.org/doc/138dd4/).

---

master thinkers. Dani Rodrik is an economist with an unusually broad interdisciplinary background. He recently returned from the Princeton School of Science to the John F. Kennedy School at Harvard. What is striking for a German academic when engaging with the work of such a renowned scholar from enormously prestigious institutions is the clarity of his argument, their interdisciplinary accessibility and practical relevance. The theorem to which we will continuously refer is the 'trilemma thesis' which Rodrik submitted in 2011.[5] He asserts the impossibility of the simultaneous pursuit of economic globalisation, democratic politics and national determination (autonomy), highlighting a trilemma in which only two goals can be paired: economic globalisation and democratic politics or democracy and national autonomy. International trade law is by no means the only field in which he illustrates his thesis, but it occupies a prominent place and is an example which lends itself to instructive comparisons of global governance arrangements and Europeanisation processes, an aspect upon which we will draw in our analysis of the TTIP.[6]

Karl Polanyi, the second mastermind upon which we rely,[7] has attracted much attention recently.[8] Although Rodrik does not cite him, his indebtedness to the Polanyian tradition is nevertheless quite readily apparent. Suffice it here to underline the historical and contextual dimensions of his analysis of trade relations, and, equally importantly, his understanding of markets as social institutions.[9]

---

[5]   Dani Rodrik, *The Globalization Paradox: Democracy and the Future of the World Economy*, Norton, New York, 2012. Rodrik summarised his argument lucidly in Dani Rodrik, "The Globalization Paradox", in *Social Europe*, 7 January 2014.

[6]   It is worth mentioning that Rodrik has added that the European Union furnishes a dramatic illustration of this: see Dani Rodrik, *The Future of European Democracy*, Princeton Institute of Advanced Studies, 2014.

[7]   Karl Polanyi, *The Great Transformation: The Political and Economic Origins of Our Time*, Beacon Press, Boston, 2001.

[8]   On Polanyi's topicality see, for example, Jens Beckert, *The Social Order of Markets*, Max Planck Institute for the Study of Societies, MPIfG Discussion Paper No. 07/15, Cologne, 2007; Wolfgang Streeck, *Re-Forming Capitalism: Institutional Change in the German Political Economy*, Oxford University Press, New York, 2009, pp. 154–156; and the *maître penseur* among the Polanyi experts: Fred Block, "Karl Polanyi and the Writing of The Great Transformation", in *Theory and Society*, 2003, vol. 32, no. 3, pp. 275–306.

[9]   See the sections from Polanyi's *Great Transformation* reprinted in Naazneen H. Barma and Steven K. Vogel (eds.), *The Political Economy Reader: Markets as Institutions*, Routledge, New York, 2008, pp. 121–151.

I take this latter aspect as the point of departure. Polanyi, publishing in 1944, was, of course, not dealing with the markets for sophisticated technical consumer goods, food and services, as we know them today. His notion of 'embeddedness', which captures the social and institutional environment of markets (that is, both the establishment of the legal frameworks within which markets can function, and the formal and social norms which guide their functioning) is, nonetheless, anything but outdated.[10] Polanyi's analyses focused on the three fictitious commodities – land, labour and money – which have in common that they concern goods which were not produced to be sold on markets, but were, nevertheless, 'marketed', and subjected to market governance as if they were regular commodities. With regard to these three fictitious commodities, 'embeddedness' denotes a precarious constellation. The politically imposed commodification of the three fictitious commodities cannot be expected to be accomplished easily; instead, such 'political' moves will spark crises and provoke counter-movements – an insight of discomfiting topicality.[11] The notion of 'embeddedness' is of general importance and is applicable to the economy as a whole.[12] There is more than a kernel of truth in this insight. We only need to open our eyes and see: markets do not function like machines; economic modelling tends to neglect what economic sociologists emphasise, namely, the moralisation and politicisation of market processes.[13] We have to understand "markets as polities".[14]

This is why, in order to function, markets require the establishment of institutional frameworks, and these frameworks must respond to conflicts. Contestation over matters other than price is an inherent dimension

---

[10] See, for a recent re-construction of the whole tradition, Fred Block and Margaret Somers, *The Power of Market Fundamentalism: Karl Polanyi's Critique*, Harvard University Press, Cambridge, 2014.

[11] See Christian Joerges, "Law and Politics in Europe's Crisis: On the History of the Impact of an Unfortunate Configuration", in *Constellations*, 2014, vol. 21, no. 2, pp. 249–261.

[12] Sabine Frerichs, "Re-embedding Neo-liberal Constitutionalism: A Polanyian Case for the Economic Sociology of Law", in Christian Joerges and Josef Falke (eds.), *Karl Polanyi: Globalisation and the Potential of Law in Transnational Markets*, Hart Publishing, Oxford, 2011, pp. 65–84.

[13] Nico Stehr, *Die Moralisierung der Märkte: eine Gesellschaftstheorie* [The Moralisation of the Markets: A Social Theory], Suhrkamp Verlag, Frankfurt, 2007.

[14] Christian Joerges, Bo Stråth and Peter Wagner (eds.), *The Economy as a Polity: The Political Constitution of Contemporary Capitalism*, UCL Press, London, 2005.

of markets. This implies that a well-functioning system of dispute resolution is a competitive advantage in international arenas.[15]

If all this holds true for the markets of consolidated polities, how can it be otherwise in the post-national constellation of international trade. It cannot, in principle, but it poses more and challenging problems. They are two-fold. For one, both if and because markets in the real world synthesise cultural orientations and political contestation, their institutionalisation will differ from one polity to another. This is a finding which studies on the varieties of capitalism, as initiated in 2011 by Peter Hall and David Soskice, have validated time and again.[16] It implies that the ordering of markets will not be uniform, prompting a challenge of a normative kind: Which ordering is to prevail? Who is legitimated to decide upon the conflict constellations ensuing from such diversities? Polanyi's perception of these challenges is simply amazing. He spells out normative challenges and implications which hardly anybody in the varieties of capitalism school has articulated.[17] The pertinent passage deserves to be cited in full:

> [W]ith the disappearance of the automatic mechanism of the gold standard, governments will find it possible to [...] tolerate willingly that other nations shape their domestic institutions according to their inclinations, thus transcending the pernicious nineteenth century dogma of the necessary uniformity of domestic regimes within the orbit of world economy. Out of the ruins of the Old World, cornerstones of the New can be seen to emerge: economic collaboration of governments *and* the liberty to organize national life at will.[18]

What Polanyi submits is a vision of transnational ordering which synthesises the functional necessities of international markets with the normative concerns prevailing in the participating polities. This is precisely what international trade law should seek to accomplish.

---

[15] This illustrates that HiiL's focus on innovating justice is not esoteric, but instead concerns a key feature of societies.

[16] Peter A. Hall and David Soskice, "An Introduction to Varieties of Capitalism", in Peter A. Hall and David Soskice (eds.), *Varieties of Capitalism: Institutional Foundations of Comparative Advantage*, Oxford University Press, Oxford, 2001, pp. 1–68.

[17] With the notable exception of Streeck, 2009, see *supra* note 8, pp. 246 ff.

[18] Polanyi, 2001, see *supra* note 7, pp. 253–254.

2.2. The Trilemma: Tensions between Deep Economic Integration, Democratic Legitimacy, and Political Autonomy

In my view, Rodrik's work on globalisation serves to elaborate upon and defend Polanyi's 'trilemma thesis' in that his argument derives from, or is based upon, the latter. The autonomy of polities is curtailed if they are compelled, in the name of free trade, to accept standards or other prescriptions which do not mirror their own preferences – economic integration and national self-determination do not go hand in hand. A resolution of this conflict is conceivable through the establishment of a transnational level. What is inconceivable, however, is the establishment of democratic decision-making which would reflect and implement some common will of all members of the WTO. The 'trilemma thesis' does not dictate that a commitment to democracy implies that we must forego the economic advantages of free trade – its message, instead, is that we ought to be aware of the tensions between free trade, diversity of socio-economic conditions and political orientations, and the quest for the legitimacy of transnational decision-making. We cannot resolve the trilemma, but we can search for economically-sound and normatively fair compromises. This is the springboard for Rodrik's re-construction of the development of the international trade system, an illuminating perspective indeed.

2.2.1. International Trade in the Era of 'Embedded Liberalism'

Rodrik's key witness and main theoretical ally is another *maître penseur* from the Kennedy School of Government at Harvard University with broad theoretical *Bildung*, albeit one who highlights the indebtedness of this approach to Polanyi openly: in a seminal study, John Gerard Ruggie characterised the post-war period of the GATT, the Bretton Woods System, and the foundational period of the (then) European Economic Community, as the age of a politically and socially "embedded liberalism".[19] The validity of Ruggie's analysis, and the adequacy of the notion that he coined, remains uncontested. Its importance for our argument should be obvious: both post-war trade regimes, the GATT and the European Economic Committee, established frameworks which left "the participating states with very

---

[19] John G. Ruggie, "International Regimes, Transactions and Change: Embedded Liberalism in the Postwar Economic Order", in *International Organization*, 1982, vol. 36, no. 2, pp. 375–415; see Jens Steffek, *Embedded Liberalism and its Critics: Justifying Global Governance in the American Century*, Palgrave Macmillan, New York, 2006.

considerable freedoms to pursue their regulatory objectives and distributional policies". This latter conclusion is Rodrik's, who deserves to be cited at some length, since two of the arguments of this chapter rely to a large degree on his analysis:[20]

> The considerable manoeuvring room afforded by these trading rules allowed advanced nations to build customized versions of capitalism around distinct approaches to corporate governance, labour markets, tax regimes, business-government relations, and welfare state arrangements. What emerged in a phrase coined by the political scientists Peter Hall and David Soskice, were 'varieties of capitalism'.[21] The United States, Britain, France, Germany, or Sweden were each market-based economies, but the institutions that underpinned their markets differed substantially and bore unmistakably national characteristics.

These conclusions contrast markedly with the oft-repeated critique of the insufficiencies of the GATT system, and the praise of the more comprehensive scope and the more rigid juridification which was then accomplished by the WTO in 1994. Both Rodrik and Ruggie underline that this agreement achieved a deepening of economic integration.[22] They add, however, that this achievement came at a price. The autonomy of nation-states and the toleration of their political preferences were severely curtailed. The reasons for such are explored in the next section.

2.2.2. The Move from the GATT to the WTO: Reasons and Challenges

In the final sections of his famous article, Ruggie discusses in depth the advent of new challenges to the balancing of national autonomy and international economic integration in the era of 'embedded liberalism'. Under the GATT regime, objections to free trade were essentially economic, and tariffs were a nation-state's primary means of protecting its interests. By the early 1970s, tariffs had been substantially reduced – in this respect, the GATT was remarkably successful. However, what the trade community

---

[20] Rodrik, 2011, see *supra* note 7, p. 74.

[21] Hall and Soskice (eds.), 2001, see *supra* note 16.

[22] John G. Ruggie, "Globalization and the Embedded Liberalism Compromise: The End of an Era?", Max Planck Institute for the Study of Societies, MPIfG Working Paper No. 97/1, Cologne, 1997.

witnessed was a steady increase of so-called 'non-tariff barriers' to trade. These barriers reflected a wide range of domestic concerns about the protection of health, safety, and the environment. They became the crucially important issues in the bargaining over trade agreements and their implementation. Ruggie's remarks on these new obstacles to free trade are anything but hostile. He acknowledges that these developments both represent and further a new type of 'social embeddedness' of markets. They also created new challenges for the international trade system as a whole, however. Domestic regulatory objectives that are generally embedded in a nation state's legal system, sometimes at a constitutional level, were now confronted with 'external' objections as to both their regulatory reasonableness and their protectionist implications. Ruggie, writing in 1982, could not predict that the international trade system would adapt to this new constellation a decade later by transforming the GATT into the WTO, an institutional move which created more effective means for dispute resolution and included a number of special Agreements (such as the Agreement on the Application of Sanitary and Phytosanitary Measures and the Agreement on Technical Barriers to Trade), with rules for balancing the economic concerns of free trade with the social concerns of regulatory objectives.

The ambiguities of these developments are readily apparent. The non-tariff barriers to trade reflected new concerns for the health and safety of consumers, and for the protection of the environment. This move to greater 'social regulation' responded to legitimate concerns and had a democratic basis. The new challenge was the defence of these credentials at the transnational level. The same phenomenon could, of course, also be observed in Europe – and Europe developed innovative and promising responses to the new challenge. Europe's dedication to the "completion of the internal market" from the 1980s onwards was accompanied by the establishment of an impressive range of transnationally operating regulatory responses: a reform of the committee system ('comitology') which was particularly important in the food markets, the invention of a "new approach to technical harmonisation and standards", the establishment of European agencies, and the promotion of the "Open Method of Co-ordination" by the Lisbon Council of the year 2000.

None of these responses was without technical problems or normative flaws. However, they had in common the search for legitimacy through procedural requirements, which were to ensure the deliberative quality of decision-making processes and the fairness of their outcome.[23]

In their institutional design and in the processes of decision-making, the legitimacy of the European responses was never uncontested. Yet, in each case, it was possible to discern a response to valid legitimacy concerns. Thus, in the case of 'comitology', a notion of 'deliberative supranationalism' – one supported by the author of this essay[24] – postulated legitimacy for this institution in its mandatory procedural requirements, which secured the normative quality of a co-operative search for solutions to common problems. Equally, in the case of agencies, the experiences of the US provide us with ample instruction on how to compensate for the potential dissolution of the separation of powers through the establishment of new institutional forms of pluralist accountability,[25] and how to exclude agency governance from spheres of re-distributive politics in which majoritarian legitimacy seemed indispensable.[26] The 'Open Method of Co-ordination' was less legalised, but its advocates similarly insisted that it was deserving of recognition as a form of 'experimentalist democracy'.[27] For a good number of years, it seemed conceivable that the European experience could orient the further development of transnational governance arrangements in the international trade system. Such visions turned out to be overly optimistic for two reasons.

One is internal to the European Union ('EU'): the sheer number of decisional issues that must be resolved, only increasing dramatically with

---

23 See, in much detail, Christian Joerges and Michelle Everson, "Re-conceptualising Europeanisation as a Public Law of Collisions: Comitology, Agencies and an Interactive Public Adjudication", in Herwig C.H. Hofmann and Alexander H. Türk (eds.), *EU Administrative Governance*, Edward Elgar Publishing, Cheltenham, 2006, pp. 512–540. In this section, I frequently cite my own work as it serves the purpose of brevity to do so.

24 Christian Joerges and Jürgen Neyer, "From Intergovernmental Bargaining to Deliberative Political Processes: The Constitutionalisation of Comitology", in *European Law Journal*, 2002, vol. 3, no. 3, pp. 273–299.

25 See Michelle Everson, "Independent Agencies: Hierarchy Beaters?", in *European Law Journal*, 1995, vol. 1, no. 1, pp. 180–204.

26 Giandomenico Majone, "The European Community between Social Policy and Social Regulation", in *Journal of Common Market Studies*, 1993, vol. 31, no. 2, pp. 153–170.

27 Charles F. Sabel and Jonathan Zeitlin, "Learning from Difference: The New Architecture of Experimentalist Governance in the EU", in *European Law Journal*, 2008, vol. 14, no. 3, pp. 271–327.

the Eastern enlargement of the EU and becoming ever more complicated due to its continually deepening socio-economic and political diversity, fostered a turn to politically unaccountable technocratic problem-solving.[28] In this process, the attractiveness of the European example has eroded.[29]

The second reason is specific to transnational governance constellations. Europe could build upon its institutional framework and its well-elaborated procedures of decision-making – constructs which are simply not in place in the international trade system. The 'softness' of international trade law mirrors, by the same token, the heterogeneity of the WTO members. The degree of uniformity which Europe continues to find worth striving for is inconceivable in the international system. The logic of this system is of a different kind. The first option it tried was a reduction of the complexity of trade conflict constellation through a one-dimensional free trade reading of the mandate of the WTO. This strategy was bound to fail because trade law experienced the rise of competing regimes which responded to further, more comprehensive and more refined regulatory concerns. The second, by now clearly prevailing, strategy is a highly meticulous type of reasoning which turns every argument around twice and seeks thereby to camouflage the precarious legitimacy of transnational decision-making. The outcome of these endeavours is, at times, admirable. One can discern in highly controversial and politically sensitive fields, such as the legendary hormones case,[30] an avoidance of definite decisions and a channelling of further

---

[28] Maria Weimer, *Constitutionalising EU Administrative Risk Governance – A Case Study of GMO Authorisations*, Oxford University Press, Oxford, forthcoming; Christian Joerges and Jürgen Neyer, "Deliberativer Supranationalismus in der Krise" [Deliberative Supranationalism in Crisis], in Oliver Flugel-Martinsen, *et al.* (eds.), *Deliberative Kritik – Kritik der Deliberation* [Deliberative Criticism – Critique of Deliberation], *Festschrift für Rainer Schmalz-Bruns*, Springer VS, Wiesbaden, 2014, pp. 353–372; more optimistically, Emilia Korkea-aho, *Adjudicating New Governance: Deliberative Democracy in the EU*, Routledge, London, 2015.

[29] See in much detail Josef Falke and Christian Joerges (eds.), *Handelsliberalisierung und Sozialregulierung in transnationalen Konstellationen* [Trade Liberalisation and Social Regulation in Transnational Constellations], Nomos, Baden-Baden, 2013; Christian Joerges and Carola Glinski (eds.), *The European Crisis and the Transformation of Transnational Governance: Authoritarian Managerialism versus Democratic Governance*, Hart Publishing, Oxford, 2014.

[30] World Trade Organization Appellate Body Report, *EC Measures Concerning Meat and Meat Products (Hormones)*, WT/DS26/AB/R and WT/DS48/AB/R, 16 January 1998 (http://www.legal-tools.org/doc/1afe89/).

deliberation.[31] In this series of cases dealing with the threats to much-loved dolphins, one can also find a patient and prudent search for fair compromises.[32] The flipside to such caution can be found in the enormous technical refinements and demands which are time consuming, costly and, nevertheless, often inconclusive. The panel report in that litigation reached the length of some 1,400 pages, most of which took great pains to explain what the panel did *not* decide, while the decision actually taken was a highly problematic imposition of time restraints on political processes within the EU.[33] This very discomfiting state of international trade law is by no means the primary reason for the efforts to now strive for comprehensive trade agreements, but it is one that should be taken into account in their evaluation.

2.3. TTIP – The Contested Consummation of Transnational Governance

The TTIP is just one, albeit the most spectacular, of many regional trade agreements that may eventualise. Negotiation on the TTIP started in 2013. While negotiations have stalled at the time of writing, they may yet culminate in a "deep and comprehensive" agreement which would reduce tariffs barriers further, and open up markets on services, investments, public procurement, as expected. The reasons for the move towards agreements of this type and their external effects are manifold.[34] The following analysis is confined to the new mode of governance which the TTIP represents, or at the very least has the potential to represent, in an exemplary fashion.

---

[31] Christian Joerges, "Judicialization and Transnational Governance: The Example of WTO Law and the GMO Dispute", in Bogdan Iancu (ed.), *The Law/Politics Distinction in Contemporary Public Law Adjudication*, Eleven International Publishing, Utrecht, 2009, pp. 67–84.

[32] World Trade Organization Appellate Body Report, *Measures Concerning the Importation, Marketing and Sale of Tuna and Tuna Products*, WT/DS381/AB/R, 16 May 2012 (http://www.legal-tools.org/doc/77380f/).

[33] Alexia Herwig and Christian Joerges, "The Precautionary Principle in Conflicts-law Perspectives", in Geert Van Calster and Denise Prévost (eds.), *Research Handbook on Environment, Health and the WTO*, Edward Elgar Publishing, Cheltenham, 2013, pp. 3–40.

[34] The accompanying debate is intense and multi-faceted. Suffice it here to mention the quasi officious presentation by Alberto Alemanno, *The Transatlantic Trade and Investment Partnership (TTIP) and Parliamentary Regulatory Cooperation*, European Parliament Policy Report, Brussels, 2014.

Among these aspects is the public inaccessibility of the negotiations. The fierce public critique has led the European Commission, "as part of its ongoing efforts to make its negotiations with the US the most open and transparent trade talks to date", to launch a public online consultation on investor protection in the TTIP.[35] This is an important concession. But it cannot camouflage the discrepancy between regular legislative procedures and the logic of international negotiations in which transparency bears with it specific risks for successful completion.[36] Rodrik observes that "[w]e cherish our democracy and national sovereignty, and yet we sign one trade agreement after another". The dilemma returns in the main objective of the TTIP. There has been much critical talk about an assumed American interest to sell chlorine-washed chicken to Europeans. The underlying assumption that European regulatory prescriptions are stricter than American standards is unfounded; even the assumed benefits of Europe's commitment to the precautionary principle are questionable.[37] But this is not the crux of the matter. The barrier which the TTIP would seek to overcome is the difficulty of arriving at 'positive' regulatory responses rather than an assessment of the legitimacy of this or that restraint. The TTIP is envisioned as a proactive agreement. Regulators on both sides of the Atlantic would be expected to engage in a 'bilateral mechanism': at the request of one party, they would start a bilateral exchange regarding the proposed policy activities. Furthermore, and more importantly, the TTIP is intended to establish a "Regulatory Cooperation Council", composed of experts who would work towards regulatory harmonisation.[38] Would this lead to agreements on the lowest common denominator, or instead to 'learning' and 'better regulation' for the benefit of all? Like the common European monetary policy, one rule may not really fit either side. What we can predict for sure is that regulatory autonomy would be restricted and democratic processes outlawed by transnational law. Again, we observe a shift of policy-making activities to the anonymous circles which cannot but operate technocratically.

---

[35] European Commission, "European Commission launches public online consultation on investor protection in TTIP", 27 March 2014.

[36] See Fernanda G. Nicola, "The Paradox of Transparency: The Politics of Regulatory Cooperation in the TTIP Negotiation", in *SidiBlog*, 4 February 2015.

[37] Cass R. Sunstein, "Precautions against What? The Availability Heuristic and Cross-Cultural Risk Perceptions", in *John M. Olin Law & Economics Working Papers*, No. 220, 2004.

[38] Marija Bartl, "TTIP's Regulatory Cooperation and The Politics Of 'Learning'", in *Social Europe*, 26 November 2015.

We can be confident that the length of the TTIP would exceed that of the CETA with its 1,400 pages. We can also be sure of the need to supplement or to revise the regulatory approaches and standards therein. The TTIP must indeed be a living agreement – whose life will be filled by technocratic expertise.[39]

The TTIP's most controversial innovation is the investor-state dispute resolution. Investments on the other side of the Atlantic must not be de-valued without further ado by measures of the host state. An arbitration tribunal composed of judges appointed by the parties will examine the justification of such measures and eventually impose compensation. This is not new in principle. Some 2,860 bilateral investment treaties, together with 339 other international investment agreements are already in place.[40] So far, they have been meant to protect and attract investors in less developed countries.[41] None of the justifications given for this *praxis* applies in the EU-US relationship.[42]

A seemingly compelling logic underlies these developments: markets will always be regulated and 'socially embedded'. This holds true for both national and international markets. The latter, alas, must search for an alternative to the kind of legitimate rule that we know from consolidated democracies. This is why we face a 'trilemma'. The 'trilemma' cannot be resolved. But there is room for manoeuvre and compromise. Can we hope for

---

[39] See for a detailed instructive analysis Josef Falke, *Hohe Standards beibehalten und nicht-tarifäre Handelshemmnisse abbauen. (Wie) geht beides?* [Maintain High Standards and Reduce Non-Tariff Trade Barriers: (How) About Both?], Centre of European Law and Politics, University of Bremen.

[40] United Nations Conference on Trade and Development, *World Investment Report 2013: Global Value Chains: Investment and Trade for Development*, United Nations, Geneva, 2013, p. 101.

[41] See, for a critical account, David Schneiderman, *Constitutionalizing Economic Globalization: Investment Rules and Democracy's Promise*, Cambridge University Press, Cambridge, 2008; David Schneiderman, *Resisting Economic Globalization: Critical Theory and International Investment Law*, Palgrave Macmillan, London, 2013; David Schneiderman, "The Global Regime of Investor Rights: Return to the Standards of Civilised Justice?", in *Transnational Legal Theory*, 2014, vol. 5, no. 1, pp. 60–80.

[42] See Pia Eberhardt, "Investment Protection at a Crossroads: The TTIP and the Future of International Investment Law", in *Dialogue on Globalization*, Friedrich-Ebert-Stiftung, Berlin, 2014, and the many contributions to the symposium "A Critical View on Investment Protection in TTIP", organised by Isabel Feichtner and Markus Krajewski, available on *Verfassungsblog*.

mutual gains and rely upon 'output legitimacy'? This seems unlikely; at best, it is highly uncertain. Will the TTIP impress the People's Republic of China and protect us against their expansionist economic policy through a bulk of standards which non-Atlantic countries cannot adhere to, or at least not influence? This may be the hidden agenda of the TTIP. It would be one which by no means sustains the legitimacy of the TTIP project. Under the prevailing conditions of uncertain economic gains and certain normative losses, it seems advisable to slow down economic globalisation in favour of national autonomy and democratic decision-making. To cite a formula which documents Rodrik's realism, theoretical background and normative assumptions: we have to realise that "the scope of workable global regulation limits the scope of desirable globalisation".[43] Rodrik recently added that, "[t]here is no need to fret about deglobalisation. Politicians should focus on restoring the domestic social contract".[44] To come back to the beginning:[45]

> Instead of decrying people's stupidity and ignorance in rejecting trade deals, we should try to understand why such deals lost legitimacy in the first place. I'd put a large part of the blame on mainstream elites and trade technocrats who poohpoohed ordinary people's concerns with earlier trade agreements.

---

[43] Rodrik, 2012, see *supra* note 5, p. 323.

[44] Dani Rodrik, "There is no need to fret about deglobalisation", in *Financial Times*, 4 October 2016.

[45] Dani Rodrik, "The Wallonia Mouse and Undemocratic Trade Deals", in *Social Europe*, 25 October 2016.

3

The Role of Transnational Private Regulation in Global Governance

Andrea Renda and Fabrizio Cafaggi*

Private players have always interacted with public authorities in the design and implementation of legal rules and standards.[1] From the Law Merchant in medieval times, to the emergence of large international standard-setting organisations during the twentieth century, privately-set rules and standards started to cross borders and facilitate trade much before the birth of the modern state, and have continued to exert a substantial impact on global legal governance ever since.[2] At the same time, also at the domestic level, modern capitalism and growing industry specialization have determined the emergence of important informational asymmetries between public policy-makers and market participants, which created demand for self- and co-regulatory schemes as viable regulatory options, subject to certain preconditions.[3] Both at the domestic and transnational level, the acceleration of

---

* **Andrea Renda** is Senior Research Fellow and Head of Regulatory Policy at the Centre for European Policy Studies (CEPS) and Professor of Digital Innovation at the College of Europe in Bruges. **Fabrizio Cafaggi** is Member of the Italian Council of State.

[1] This contribution builds on research on the project of transnational private regulation carried by the authors with HiiL, the results of which are published in Fabrizio Cafaggi, *A Comparative Analysis of Transnational Private Regulation: Legitimacy, Quality, Effectiveness and Enforcement*, EUI Department of Law Research Paper No. 2014/145, 2014; and with Strijbis Foundation, the results of which are published in Fabrizio Cafaggi and Andrea Renda, *Measuring the Effectiveness of Transnational Private Regulation*, 2014.

[2] See Harold J. Berman, *Law and Revolution: The Formation of the Western Legal Tradition*, Harvard University Press, 1983, pp. 332–56 (discussing the rise of mercantile law); see also Mary Elizabeth Basile *et al.* (eds.), *Lex Mercatoria and Legal Pluralism: A Late Thirteenth-Century Treatise and Its Afterlife*, Ames Foundation, Cambridge, 1998; Fabrizio Cafaggi, "The Many Features of Transnational Private Rule Making", in *Pennsylvania Journal of International Law*, 2015, vol. 36, no. 4, p. 101.

[3] Edward Balleisen and Marc A. Eisner, "The Promise and Pitfalls of Co-Regulation: How Governments Can Draw on Private Governance for Public Purpose", in David Moss and

technological development, the growth of common resources (such as forestry and fishing stocks), increasing concerns for the environment and human rights, the growth of global value chains,[4] and the rise of new policy fields in which information is mostly in the hands of private players (such as critical infrastructure protection and global finance), are creating new demand for regulatory schemes that heavily involve private actors, or are even exclusively controlled by them.

Within the broad category of public-private regulatory co-operation, several variants can be highlighted. First, some regulatory schemes feature private players in the driving seat, that is, involved from the agenda-setting phase of policy-making, often alongside the implementation and enforcement of private rules, with no significant involvement of public policymakers. This can be due to the failure of national governments and/or international organisations to tackle an issue effectively through treaties or inter-governmental agreements, as was the case for the Kimberley Process on conflict diamonds, or for the Forest Stewardship Council after the failure of the 1982 Earth summit in Rio de Janeiro. It could also be due to an implicit or explicit decision by government to stay away from the policy field and delegate regulatory functions to private organisations, as seen in the regulation of the internet by the Internet Corporation for Assigned Names and Numbers, the Internet Engineering Task Force and the World Wide Web Consortium. In a second group of cases, private players or private organisations enter into collaborative schemes that also involve international governmental organisations.[5] This is the case of the recently created Breakthrough Energy Coalition; or that of the GAVI Alliance, in which the Bill and Melinda Gates Foundation plays a decisive role along with the World Health Organization, the United Nations ('UN') Children's Fund and the World Bank. A third group of cases includes transnational private standards that complement public regulation by focusing on the implementation of public policy, mostly by offering common solutions developed by the

---

John Cisternino (eds.), *New Perspectives on Regulation*, The Tobin Project, 2009; Fabrizio Cafaggi and Andrea Renda, *Public and Private Regulation: Mapping the Labyrinth*, CEPS Working Document, No. 370, Centre for European Policy Studies, Brussels, 2012.

[4] Gary Gereffi and Karina Fernandez-Stark, *Global Value Chain Analysis: A Primer*, Center on Globalization, Governance and Competitiveness, Duke University, Durham, 2011.

[5] See Kenneth W. Abbott *et al.*, "Two Logics of Indirect Governance: Delegation and Orchestration", in *British Journal of Political Science*, 2016, vol. 46, no. 4, pp. 719–729.

industry. This is the case of very large organisations such as the International Accounting Standards Board, or the International Swaps and Derivatives Association. A special case is the International Organization for Standardization, where standards like ISO 26000 have more recently been developed on the basis of collaborative agreements with the Organization for Economic Co-operation and Development and the International Labour Organization. Similar to these cases are co-regulatory schemes, which distinguish themselves with the existence of a 'legal backstop': examples include advertising standards developed by the European Advertising Standards Alliance, the European Payment Council set up to speed up the transition towards the Single European Payment Area, and many more.[6] Finally, transnational regulatory schemes are also abundant within global value chains, as they help multinational corporations ('MNCs') manage their contractual relationships with suppliers and customers. Standards such as GlobalG.A.P. and Utz Certified in the agri-food chain, to name just two examples, serve the purpose of reducing transaction costs and increasing the efficiency of contractual relationships, especially when viewed from the standpoint of MNCs and their local suppliers.[7]

Against this background, the existing variety in Transnational Private Regulation ('TPR') schemes is amplified by the diversity of their governance arrangements. The more TPR is seen as a suitable and often desirable alternative, or a complement, to public regulation, the greater the pressure exerted on TPR schemes to align their operations with the public interest. In line with the conclusions in other contributions in this volume, this chapter finds that all phases of the policy cycle, and in particular the enforcement and compliance phases, should be strengthened in the governance of TPR schemes to make them a suitable, effective alternative to command and control regulation. In this respect, enhanced attention by governments, civil society organisations and the public opinion has led to a number of recent trends in the field of TPR. These include a greater commingling of public and private schemes; a growing sophistication of the governance of such schemes; the birth of private 'meta-regulators' that develop standards for TPR schemes with a view to increase their credibility and legitimacy; and renewed pressure to strengthen monitoring and evaluation of the TPR

---

[6] Cafaggi, 2014, see *supra* note 1; Cafaggi and Renda, 2014, see *supra* note 1.
[7] Fabrizio Cafaggi, "The Regulatory Provisions of Transnational Commercial Contracts: New Architectures", in *Fordham Journal of International Law*, 2013, vol. 36, no. 6, p. 1557.

schemes in place, as well as their ability to secure compliance with their rules.[8]

3.1. The Operation of TPR Schemes

TPR schemes typically operate through voluntary standards subscribed by regulated entities that contractually bind their business partners to commit with their principles and rules.[9] Key dimensions of TPR schemes that are relevant from the standpoint of their effectiveness are their governance, their standard-setting procedures, the monitoring arrangements they adopt to ensure compliance and the extent to which they evaluate and communicate their results. In turn, these dimensions affect the input and output legitimacy of the TPR scheme, as well as their effectiveness.[10] Below, we touch upon each of these aspects.

3.1.1. Governance

In terms of overall governance, TPR schemes involve a multiplicity of actors such as firms, non-governmental organizations ('NGOs'), independent experts, or epistemic communities.[11] As a general trend, industries, and NGOs, despite representing conflicting interests and divergent policy objectives, increasingly engage in transnational co-operation rather than private regulatory competition. This is partly the outcome of a spontaneous process, driven by the steering activity of international organizations. As a result, multi-stakeholder organisations are replacing many single-stakeholder regulators. Many TPR schemes, especially in the domain of global governance, involve both MNCs and NGOs, and often also governments or international governmental organisations.[12] Depending on the case, TPR schemes can emerge as single or multi-stakeholder organisations;

---

[8] Fabrizio Cafaggi, "Transnational Private Regulation: Regulating Private Regulators", in Sabino Cassese (ed.), *Research Handbook on Global Administrative Law*, Edward Elgar, 2016.

[9] Cafaggi and Renda, 2014, see *supra* note 1.

[10] *Ibid.*

[11] Fabrizio Cafaggi, "New Foundations of Transnational Private Regulation", in *Journal of Law and Society*, 2011, vol. 38, no. 1, p. 20.

[12] The degree of participation of these types of actors in the so-called 'governance triangle' was mapped by Kenneth W. Abbott and Duncan Snidal, "The Governance Triangle: Regulatory Standards Institutions and the Shadow of the State", in Walter Mattli and Ngaire Woods (eds.), *The Politics of Global Regulation*, Princeton University Press, 2009, p. 44.

regardless of their governance choices, they have to solve conflicts between different constituencies within the private sphere.

Most often, TPR schemes are multi-stakeholder in nature, as they feature a high degree of heterogeneity and are normally geared towards the production of global public goods, or standards that facilitate the interaction between different types of players. In the former case, NGOs will normally be involved or even act as originators, often in co-operation with private business (for instance, the Marine Stewardship Council ('MSC') was created through an agreement between Unilever and the World Wildlife Fund in 1997). In the latter case, both suppliers and customers are often represented in the main decision-making body of the scheme. A slightly different case is found in the so-called 'expertise-based regulation' sphere, which entails significant delegation to technical standard-setting bodies, and as such tends to involve non-technical experts only in an observer role.[13] More generally, depending on the circumstances, the terms of involvement of specific types of actors can change: even when they do not sit in the main decision-making bodies of the scheme, NGOs can exert a significant influence on the scheme (for instance, by acting as internal or external evaluators of the extent to which all relevant interests are factored into the decision-making process, or even directly evaluating the outcomes and impacts generated by the scheme). Finally, some transnational organisations take the form of federations with a multi-level structure based on national bodies: this adds complexity to their governance, since national bodies are often very influential, and tend to compete in international standardisation bodies such as the International Organization for Standardization or the International Electrotechnical Commission to serve their domestic interests, rather than the global good.[14]

---

[13] Such as the International Organization for Standardization, the International Telecommunications Union, the International Electrotechnical Commission, the World Wide Web Consortium, the Codex Alimentarius Commission, just to name a few. ISO, ITU and IEC form the World Standards. See Tim Büthe and Walter Mattli, *The New Global Rulers: The Privatization of Regulation in the World Economy*, Princeton University Press, 2011.

[14] Büthe and Mattli, 2011, see *supra* note 13. ISO members are the respective national standard setters, such as the American National Standards Institute in the USA, Deutsches Institut für Normung in Germany, or the British Standards Institution. The picture is completed by numerous regional technical standard setters that provide for harmonized technical standards within a specific region. Examples are the European Committee for Standardization, the Pan-American Standards Commission, the African Organization for Standardization, and

Key factors that define the governance of TPR schemes include:

- the existence of checks and balances within the organisation between the main standard-setting body (such as a board) and the key decision-making body (so-called 'functional separation');

- the arrangements related to membership (that is, whether the organisation is membership-based);

- the scheme's inclusiveness, intended as the inclusion of all relevant stakeholders in the key standard- and decision-making bodies of the organisation, but also as the consultation of all relevant stakeholders (including non-members) during the adoption of major decision, or in the *ex post* evaluation of existing policies even when membership status is not granted;

- the for profit/not-for-profit nature of the TPR scheme, and more generally its funding sources; and

- its transparency and accountability.

3.1.2. Standard-setting Procedures

When it comes to rule-making or standard-setting procedures, the variety of practices observed in TPR schemes becomes almost intractable. From technical organisations that traditionally vote by consensus (or by raising hands), to more structured institutions with weighted majority rules and transparency obligations, to multi-stakeholder organisations with multiple chambers representing different and at times conflicting interests, almost all variants are represented. Key aspects of standard-setting that affect the overall performance and effectiveness of TPR schemes include the use of stakeholder consultation and associated standards and responsibility, the performance of *ex ante* impact assessments, and/or *ex post* evaluation of prospective/retrospective impacts of existing rules or group of rules. Clearly, the higher the degree of interest representation within the standard-setting organisation, the greater the importance of governance arrangements. When, instead, many of the interests affected by the standards lie outside of the organisation's procedural rules concerning standard-setting,

---

many others. See Panagiotis Delimatsis (ed.), *The Law, Economics and Politics of International Standardization*, Cambridge University Press, 2016.

consultation and revision become particularly crucial to make the standard legitimate and accountable.

As TPR schemes proliferate and occupy a growing regulatory space in global governance, the transparency and accountability of their regulatory process becomes increasingly important. This is demonstrated by, for instance, the pressure exerted on regulators such as Internet Corporation for Assigned Names and Numbers to increase the transparency of their regulatory process.[15] Similarly, the ISEAL Alliance imposes on its members, and includes in its credibility principles, compliance with rules on standard-setting. The consequence is that many TPR schemes end up adopting impact assessment and consultation procedures that render them more similar to a national government than to an association of private actors or a multinational enacting a code of conduct. This, in turn, shifts the attention away from the mere assessment of the performance of the TPR scheme for its members, and towards a full-fledged assessment of the social, economic, and environmental impacts of the rules and standards produced by the TPR scheme. This trend is also echoed by the growing emphasis placed by some policy-makers on non-financial reporting by large corporations, which is increasingly applied to TPR schemes.[16] As will be explained below in more detail, 'private meta-regulators' also work in the direction of strengthening reporting and evaluation practices inside TPR schemes, as testified, *inter alia*, by the 'Impacts Code' produced by the ISEAL Alliance. International organisations such as the UN's Food and Agricultural Organization have collaborated with the ISEAL Alliance and other private organisations to

---

[15] See the 'Accountability and Transparency' section of ICANN's website; Urs Gasser *et al.*, *Accountability and Transparency at ICANN: An Independent Review*, Berkman Center Research Publication No. 2010-13, 2010.

[16] In 2014, EU institutions adopted an amendment to the Accounting Directive, as regards disclosure of non-financial and diversity information by certain large undertakings and groups: see European Parliament and European Council, *Directive 2014/95/EU amending Directive 2013/34/EU*, OJEU L 330/1, 22 October 2014 (http://www.legal-tools.org/doc/3cc2bd/). In 2016, the European Commission ran a public consultation on the non-binding guidelines on methodology for reporting non-financial information following Article 2 of Directive 2014/95/EU, with the aim to collect views from stakeholders. The consultation is part of the Commission's work related to preparing non-binding guidelines on methodology for reporting non-financial information by December 2016. See European Commission, *Communication from the European Commission: Guidelines on Non-Financial Reporting (Methodology for Reporting Non-Financial Information)*, 2017/C 215/01, 5 July 2017 (http://www.legal-tools.org/doc/730f04/).

develop a sophisticated framework for evaluation, which is chiefly based on the assessment of economic, social, environmental and governance impacts.

One important aspect of the decision-making process, along with its transparency and accountability, is whether the organisation follows a 'policy cycle' approach, which entails the *ex post* evaluation of existing rules with a view to triggering learning and improved regulatory quality over time. The ability of an organisation to learn from past mistakes and use external inputs and internal assessment to strengthen its regulatory capacity is an important signal of the potential for the TPR scheme to produce socially desirable results. At the same time, it is essential that all evaluation activities are not limited to so-called 'direct impacts', such as minimising compliance costs or maximising benefits for members of the scheme; to the contrary, TPR schemes should devote efforts to capturing the ancillary, indirect impacts of their actions in social, economic and environmental terms.[17]

Evaluation of the quality and the effectiveness of the standard-setting process represents a key feature of TPR accountability. The quality of standards partly depends on the quality of the regulatory process. A process that lacks transparency and inclusiveness is likely to lead to a standard unable to achieve the public interest objectives declared in its mission statements. Indicators related to the quality of the regulatory process should be linked to those focusing on the regulatory product. That is the approach taken in our assessment tool, in which the three pillars for evaluating standard-setting include: the process, the product, and the governance of the organisation.

3.1.3. Compliance-monitoring and -enforcement

While governance and standard-setting have traditionally been at the core of the study of TPR schemes, it is important to highlight that in many circumstances these schemes have experienced a number of problems and challenges in the 'delivery' phase of their rules, and more specifically in the

---

[17] Cafaggi and Renda, 2012, see *supra* note 3; Andrea Renda *et al.*, *Assessing the Costs and Benefits of Regulation: Study for the European Commission, Secretariat General*, CEPS and Economisti Associati, Brussels, 2013; Andrea Renda "Regulatory Impact Assessment and Regulatory Policy", in OECD, *Regulatory Policy in Perspective: A Reader's Companion to the OECD Regulatory Policy Outlook 2015*, OECD Publishing, Paris, 2015.

two inter-related phases of compliance-monitoring and -enforcement. Cases in which compliance was absent or insufficient despite certification include well-known adverse events, such as the deadly fire which occurred at the SA8000-certified Ali Enterprises garment factory on 11 September 2012, claiming the lives of nearly 300 workers; revelations on unsustainable, but still MSC-certified, fisheries;[18] and the behaviour of banks in the US under the Consolidated Supervised Entities scheme right before the subprime mortgage crisis.[19] In some cases, the problem was aggravated by the fact that compliance appeared difficult, if not impossible, to verify: this was so for the Kimberley process, the effectiveness of which was heavily affected by the impossibility of fully certifying the origin of diamonds, and the ease with which conflict diamonds could be 'whitewashed'.[20]

Furthermore, analysing compliance in the context of transnational voluntary standards requires a change of perspective compared to the context of domestic mandatory standards. For the latter, criminal and administrative law provide an overall framework for enforcing private rules,[21] whereas many global standards are enacted by global regulators and subscribed to by large MNCs which are, owing to due diligence obligations, required to ensure compliance along global chains. In the context of TPR schemes, the subscription to the standard is voluntary but the compliance

---

[18] See Claire Christian *et al.*, "Questionable stewardship: A review of formal objections to MSC fisheries certifications", in *Biological Conservation*, 2013, vol. 161, pp. 10–17.

[19] Balleisen and Eisner, 2009, see *supra* note 3.

[20] Global Witness, a London-based NGO, argued that the Kimberley Process has ultimately failed to stem the flow of conflict diamonds, leading them to abandon the scheme in 2011. In 2013, the World Policy Journal published an investigative report disclosing how USD 3.5 billion minimum in KP-certified diamonds from Angola and DRC had been looted through KP-certified tax havens such as Dubai and Switzerland in collaboration with self-regulating 'KP-approved' governments and rather obscure business intermediaries. The report argued that "the real violence of the industry is whitewashed, ignored, or excluded entirely from the framework – the criminal portion of which continues to exist entirely on the periphery". See Khadija Sharife and John Grobler, "Kimberley's Illicit Process", in *World Policy Journal*, Winter 2013/2014.

[21] However, even in the context of public domestic regulation, there are voluntary programmes administered by administrative agencies. The example of environmental performance measurement by the US environmental protection agency with sustainability scorecards deployed by transnational environmental regulators is a good illustration. See Cary Coglianese and Jennifer Nash, *Beyond Compliance: Business Decision Making and the US EPA's Performance Track Programme*, Mossavar-Rahmani Center for Business and Government, John F. Kennedy School of Government, Harvard University, 2008, pp. 52 ff.

is mandatory and operates according to contract or corporate law principles. Parties joining a transnational regime commit to complying with the rules, and with the sanctions if there is non-compliance. However judicial enforcement is not the main mechanism deployed to ensure that regulated entities will comply with standards and will react to non-compliance by adopting remedial measures. Market-driven mechanisms engineered by the regulators and NGOs, and monitored by the media, play a major role in both ensuring oversight and providing reputational incentives to comply or to repair.

Evaluation instruments can be either internal to the regulator or administered by 'delegated' third parties. NGOs often independently monitor compliance by using scorecards or reporting systems where they rank regulatory performances of individual firms or supply chains. Firms also have internal compliance-monitoring mechanisms that include oversight of the supply chain. Domestic regulators monitor compliance too, often going beyond the geographic scope of their jurisdictions.[22] The effectiveness of compliance is therefore the result of the combination of multiple related mechanisms that have to be co-ordinated in order to minimise the risk of violations and its consequences. The main actors involved in the regulatory process include the regulator and independent monitors (including NGOs and the media); the regulated (such as MNCs); and independent suppliers linked to MNCs.

In this context, the understanding regarding compliance-verification and -management has changed over the past two decades.[23] From the 'auditing society' where reporting and due diligence represented the key pillars, a first important change was driven by the 'beyond compliance' approach, based on the premise that auditing and reporting is insufficient to ensure compliance with both domestic and transnational standards.[24] More recently, the notion of static compliance is being abandoned in favour of a

---

[22] Forest L. Reinhardt, "Market Failure and the Environmental Strategies of Firms: The Microeconomic Roots of Corporate Environmental Policy", in *Journal of Industrial Ecology*, 1999, vol. 3, no. 1, pp. 9–21.

[23] Neil Gunningham, "Enforcement and Compliance Strategies", in Robert Baldwin, Martin Cave and Martin Lodge (eds.), *The Oxford Handbook of Regulation*, Oxford University Press, New York, 2010, pp. 120–145.

[24] Neil Gunningham and Peter Grabowsky, *Smart Regulation: Designing Environmental Policy*, Oxford University Press, New York, 1998.

concept of 'dynamic compliance', which entails measuring improvements of regulated entities over time according to objective yet flexible indicators, whose relative weight can change depending on exogenous factors.[25] This is because compliance with standards may be achieved over many years and the evaluation has to address the progress that individual entities and the supply chain as a whole make. This is clearly the human rights approach adopted by the UN principles.[26] The 'continuous improvement' approach characterises many new standards in the area of sustainability and environment: under this approach, improvements may concern both measurable targets and the quality of the governance like the establishment and functioning of management schemes, risk management, and other tools capable of preventing and mitigating risks when they materialize. The links with non-compliance and remedies become central pillars in the continuous improvement approach.[27] Here, the focus is shifting from analysing the consequences to examining the causes of non-compliance and the remedial part that follows suit. In this respect, many TPR schemes are coming increasingly in line with the tenets of responsive regulation.[28] Under this approach, findings of non-compliance trigger actions to restore compliance or revise the process when, for example, the management system or the organisational structure reveals slacks.[29]

What are the criteria that should inspire the design of compliance programmes? The classic relationship between governance and contractual costs developed in relation to ownership can be usefully applied to compliance.[30] This implies that transnational standards compliance programmes minimise the combined costs of governance and contracting, while

---

[25] Fabrizio Cafaggi, "Compliance in transnational regulation", in Diane Moloney and Kim Stone, *Oxford Handbook of Global Policy and Transnational Administration*, Oxford University Press, forthcoming.

[26] Report of the Special Representative of the Secretary-General on the Issue of Human Rights and Transnational Corporations and Other Business Enterprises, John Ruggie, "Guiding Principles on Business and Human Rights: Implementing the United Nations 'Protect, Respect and Remedy' Framework", UN Doc. A/HRC/17/31, 21 March 2011, p. 24.

[27] Cafaggi and Miller, 2016, see *supra* note 25.

[28] Kenneth W. Abbott and Duncan Snidal, "Taking responsive regulation transnational: Strategies for international organizations", in *Regulation and Governance*, 2012, vol. 7, no. 1.

[29] Cafaggi and Miller, 2016, see *supra* note 25.

[30] Henry Hansmann, *The Ownership of Enterprise*, Harvard University Press, Cambridge, 1996.

maximising effectiveness of oversight and improvement over the time of regulatory performance. Compliance design faces the choice among three forms of control: direct hierarchical control, peer control by the group of regulated entities, and individually-delegated control by each regulated entity. Each type of control entails costs, but of different kinds: some are organisational costs, others transactional. The most difficult design question is how different monitoring mechanisms should be combined.[31]

The most important transformation is still underway and it concerns the shift of focus towards regulatory objectives. Private regulators should design their monitoring system to ensure compliance with the objectives enshrined in the standards or by the evaluation instruments defined therein. Measuring compliance with the rules does not provide regulators and affected communities with relevant information on whether the standard achieves the objective, such as whether the environment is more protected, product safety is higher, privacy is ensured, and data circulated safely. More broadly, the question of whether the proclaimed public interest of private regulation is effectively pursued or a 'hidden private benefits search' permeates standard-implementation.

3.2. Potential Issues with TPR Schemes

Evaluation of TPR schemes concerns regulatory performance and can be carried out within benchmarking schemes or in relation to individual regulators. One of the rationales for this evaluation lies in the possible difference between private incentives and goals of TPR schemes on the one hand; and public policy goals on the other. In particular, the notion of effectiveness used by scholars or policy-makers (that is, the extent to which private regulatory schemes achieve socially optimal or desirable outcomes)[32] might well differ from the one sought by private actors involved in private regulatory schemes. Occasionally, these two notions can coincide; but in many instances they may diverge – hence the scepticism of many social scientists

---

[31] Cafaggi and Miller, 2016, see *supra* note 25.

[32] This is why effectiveness is normally linked to explicitly-stated general, specific and operational objectives in the *ex ante* impact assessments of the European Commission. The specification of objectives has become much more common in Commission impact assessments over the past few years, and the Communication on smart regulation of October 2010 placed even more emphasis on the need to define 'SMART' objectives in *ex ante* policy appraisal documents, so that achievement of those objectives can be monitored over time, including in *ex post* evaluation.

and policy-makers when it comes to evaluating private regulation. Cases in which 'private' and 'social' effectiveness diverge can be of different types: collective action in private regulatory bodies can aim at socially sub-optimal outcomes (as in the case of cartels); the TPR scheme might generate negative externalities (for example, GlobalG.A.P. has been accused of creating barriers to trade for developing countries); the scope of the private regulatory scheme might be narrower than the impact generated by its participants' activity (for example, safety-oriented certification schemes might generate unintended environmental consequences); or there might be cases in which the private regulatory scheme is aimed at achieving socially desirable outcomes, but either adverse selection problems or lack of monitoring and compliance leads to the emergence of socially undesirable outcomes.[33] Recent problems experienced by co-regulatory schemes at the EU level (notably, in payments and in data protection) have been overshadowed by the growing 'horse meat' scandal, which now extends to some of the largest producers of meat in the world, and is attributed to a joint failure of public regulation and private regulatory schemes in charge of auditing and inspecting outlets, thus complementing public regulation in the enforcement phase.

This potential misalignment between private benefits and social welfare can be dealt with by designing appropriate indicators that would make *ex ante* clear when regulatory choices pursue one or the other strategy. This could lead to the use of regulatory governance indicators, indicators related to regulatory objectives, performance indicators, and so on. In addition, it would be important to note whether a given TPR scheme is likely to maintain its virtuous features over time. As a matter of fact, besides these

---

[33] Cafaggi and Renda, 2012, see *supra* note 3. For an example, see Michael Lennox and Jennifer Nash, "Self-Regulation and Adverse Selection: A Comparison Across Four Trade Association Programs", in *Business Strategy and Environment*, 2003, vol. 12, no. 6, p. 343. Therein, Lennox and Nash describe the 'Responsible Care' initiative launched by the Chemical Manufacturer's Association in 1989 in response to growing public criticism of the industry. The fact that the Association did not require third party review or certification of firm performance and did not adopt explicit sanctions for non-compliance led to a perverse situation in which participants in Responsible Care were more polluting on average than other chemical firms in the US. Similarly, Morgenstern and Pizer, in reviewing a number of voluntary programmes in the environmental field, express concern on the self-selection of participants into those schemes, see Richard D. Morgenstern and William A. Pizer (eds.), *Reality Check, the Nature and Performance of Voluntary Environmental Programs in the United States, Europe, and Japan. Resources for the Future*, Washington, D.C., 2007.

'genetic problems', a number of other effects can undermine the alignment between private benefits and social goals during the life of a private regulatory body. These are briefly listed below:

- *Lock-in effects and collective action problems* can occur when members remain locked into sub-optimal agreements and 'focal points', with no incentive to change;
- *Path dependency, status quo bias, anchoring and framing effects* may lead to shifting focus towards measurable and immediate benefits rather than long-term social welfare;
- *Hard-to-detect changes* over time might be induced by the prevalence of some interests over others during the life of the private regulatory body (as in the case of MSC);
- *Divergence of interests* between the regulators and the regulated, which lead the former to prefer short-term actions that maximise their likelihood of being re-appointed;
- *Self-indulgence in the evaluation* of private regulatory bodies, when governance arrangements entail self-evaluation, or lack of legitimacy of third parties in charge of evaluation.

All these problems deserve careful scrutiny before one can actually conclude that a given policy issue is a good candidate for efficient and socially-effective private regulation.[34] What is still missing is a comprehensive theoretical framework for assessing TPR from the standpoint of public policy, during *ex ante* impact assessments or *ex post* sectoral screenings.[35] We have developed an evaluation framework along a number of sequential steps.[36] Initially, the evaluation should consider the origin and type of TPR by identifying the rationales for creating the scheme (if already existing) and the phases of the policy cycle covered by TPR (such as agenda-setting,

---

[34] For example, see Simon Ashby *et al.*, *Industry Self-Regulation: A Game-Theoretic Typology of Strategic Voluntary Compliance*, Financial Services Authority Working Paper, London, 2004. Ashby *et al.* distinguished a number of voluntary regulatory schemes in the United Kingdom based on the different context in which they emerge, which in turn determines a different mode of strategic interaction between private players. Accordingly, they define the United Kingdom's advertising Code as an "assurance game", its press as a "chicken game" and its life insurance as a "prisoner's dilemma".

[35] Such a framework has been provided for public regulation and regulatory policy, see Cary Coglianese, *Measuring regulatory performance: Evaluating the impact of regulation and regulatory policy*, Organisation for Economic Cooperation and Development, Paris, 2012.

[36] Cafaggi and Renda, 2014, see *supra* note 1.

rule formulation, standards, implementation, monitoring, and enforcement). Second, the evaluation of TPR should hinge on whether the governance of the TPR scheme can guarantee sufficient alignment between private benefits and social welfare: this might include the use of indicators such as participation, materiality, completeness, diversity of funding, specific governance arrangements, internal use of indicators and existence of self-evaluation or external evaluation arrangements.[37] Finally, evaluators should assess how the arrangements identified affect the quality, legitimacy and actual enforcement of the TPR scheme at hand.[38]

3.3. Harnessing the Potential of TPR Schemes in Addressing Key Societal Challenges

TPR schemes are as pervasive as they are neglected in global governance. Not only do they create rules and standards that shape the global business community and its impact on key social, environmental and economic indicators, they also chiefly influence the effectiveness of public rules by introducing standards and compliance patterns that interact with rules designed by public bodies. They increasingly constitute the vital fluid of global value chains, and are an essential vehicle of rule-making and implementation in fields where the remit of public regulators is geographically and technologically challenged. The rise of TPR schemes as a dominant method of addressing global governance issues, including in particular sustainable development issues, should not however be taken as a sign of unequivocal success, and has rightly been accompanied by a gradually more sophisticated scholarship, as well as enhanced attention from civil society.

Today, both the opportunities and the challenges are clear. The challenge is increasing the legitimacy, credibility and overall effectiveness of these schemes by improving their governance, standard-setting procedures and compliance-monitoring activities, and securing their delivery on key indicators of effectiveness. The key opportunity is fully integrating TPR in international regulatory co-operation schemes aimed at tackling the most

---

[37] For an example of a paper that uses indicators to assess the existence of such preconditions, see Doris Fuchs and Agni Kalfagianni, "The Causes and Consequences of Private Food Governance", in *Business and Politics*, 2010, vol. 12, no. 3, Article 5.

[38] Cafaggi and Renda, 2012, see *supra* note 3; Cafaggi and Renda, 2014, see *supra* note 1.

important societal problems.[39] Effective forms of public and private international co-operation may contribute to improving both TPR legitimacy and effectiveness. Orchestration schemes that involve both public and private players[40] could prove very important in this respect, but only if well-designed and governed, such that accountability and effectiveness are preserved. Examples of orchestration schemes include the GAVI Alliance, the Global Environment Facility, and the Global e-Sustainability Facility. However, these co-operative arrangements need to become more structured in terms of the definition of objectives and the measurement of their achievement. What is crucial is the process of standard-implementation that may take different routes depending on whether public entities (that is, states) or private ones (that is, supply chains) are deployed.

In this respect, key global initiatives such as the new UN Sustainable Development Goals ('SDG') signed by 193 countries in September 2015 and the Paris COP21 Agreement of February 2016 chiefly depend on the involvement of private schemes, both individually and within public-private partnerships.[41] The SDG agenda for 2030 was set up with an increased attention towards "an intensive global engagement in support of implementation of all the Goals and targets, bringing together Governments, the private sector, civil society, the United Nations system and other actors and mobilising all available resources".[42] A recent report by the UN Industrial Development Organization reflects on the need for enhanced co-operation with the private sector in realising the post-2015 sustainable development strategy of the UN, as shown in Figure 1 below.[43] Some countries have

---

[39] Organisation for Economic Cooperation and Development, *International Regulatory Co-operation: The Role of International Organisations in Fostering Better Rules of Globalisation*, OECD Publishing, Paris, 2016.

[40] Abbott *et al.*, 2015, see *supra* note 5.

[41] Oscar Widerberg and Philipp Pattberg, "Accountability Challenges in the Transnational Regime Complex for Climate Change", in *Review of Policy Research*, vol. 34, no. 1, 2016.

[42] United Nations General Assembly, "Transforming our world: the 2030 Agenda for Sustainable Development", UN Doc. A/RES/70/1, 21 October 2015, para. 39 (http://www.legal-tools.org/doc/d52143/).

[43] United Nations Industrial Development Organization and the United Nations Global Compact, *Engaging with the Private Sector in the Post-2015 Agenda: Consolidated Report on 2014 Consultations*, 2016 (http://www.legal-tools.org/doc/9e98ce/).

proposed that the UN incorporate a reporting initiative within the SDG framework, similar to the EU's non-financial reporting directive.

POST-2015 BUSINESS ENGAGEMENT ARCHITECTURE

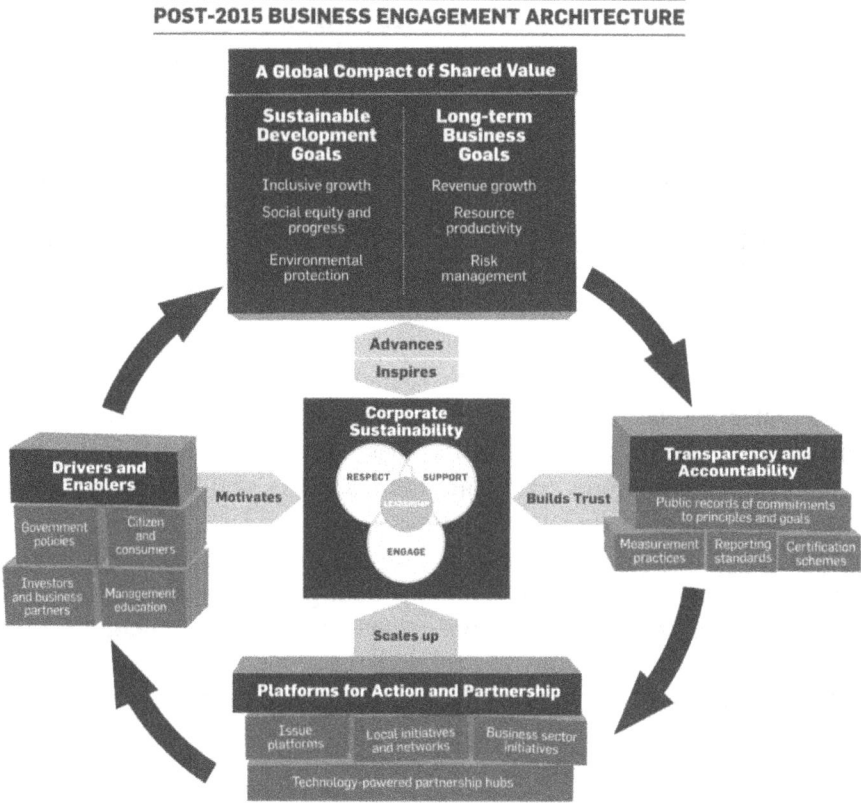

Source: United Nations Global Compact

Figure 1.

Recently, the UN also launched the so-called 'SDG compass', which outlines five steps for companies to maximize their contribution to the global SDG goals – understanding the SDGs, defining priorities, setting goals, then integrating, reporting and communicating on them. These five steps incorporate many of the lessons drawn from decades of TPR.

Likewise, and even more explicitly, implementation of the Paris COP21 Accords signed in November 2015 will only be feasible with adequate participation of the private sector. Schemes such as the Breakthrough

Energy Coalition will provide an important element in what could increasingly look like an orchestration scheme aimed at delivering on climate goals. However, it is important to avoid problems that have already emerged in similar orchestration schemes partly involving the same actors, for example the GAVI Alliance, which coupled unequivocal achievements with stark criticisms on an alleged misalignment between private incentives and public goals.

In summary, TPR schemes must be subject to smarter scrutiny and enhanced attention by public authorities and civil society, including *ad hoc* NGOs, so that they can fully deliver on their promises. More specifically, implementing dedicated guidance on how to assess private governance schemes would lead TPR to obtain full citizenship in the area of international regulatory co-operation. In this respect, TPR can prove decisive in its contributions by achieving a multi-stakeholder 'deepening' of inter-governmental commitments, thus transforming them into concrete ways to achieve progress towards politically-agreed goals on a global scale. Areas such as global commons, protecting human rights and, overall, achieving sustainability in global economic activities are perfect candidates for testing the reliability and effectiveness of public-private interplay in international regulatory co-operation, for the global good. Our analysis suggests that testing such reliability requires enhanced attention to the governance of these schemes, their ability to deal with the implementation of standards and rules, and the related degree of compliance and overall alignment with their stated long-term goals.

4

Order with Justice:
The Challenge for Global Governance*

Abiodun Williams**

4.1. Introduction

It is often said that contemporary politics and strategizing are too much concerned with crisis management and short-term pressures, and too little with the need for effecting normative change that can make a lasting difference. If our politics and strategies are enveloped by such clouds of cynicism, we need to breathe the bold, enterprising spirit of reform, driven by ideas as well as idealism. Addressing the challenge outlined in this chapter requires a level of boldness because the theme of 'order with justice' is a grand one. When applied to no less a question than 'the challenge for Global Governance', its grandeur is matched only by its topicality. As a starting point, it is important to explain the choice of such an ambitious task in view of the current international environment, not least the state of international law and its institutions.

While a just international order ought to be a consistent aspiration, detached from the circumstances of any one age, it is clear that order with justice is an especially urgent imperative in our own times, which are marked by fragility and volatility on the one hand, and the inertia and ineffectiveness of existing global governance mechanisms and instruments on the other. Whether we consider the continuing civil war in Syria, the current refugee crisis, the annexation of Ukrainian territory by Russia, the resurgence of the Israeli-Palestinian conflict or the ongoing and often under-

---

* The present chapter builds on the Marchant Lecture delivered by the author at the Hans van Mierlo Stichting in Amsterdam on 13 November 2014.

** Dr. **Abiodun Williams** is Director of the Institute for Global Leadership and Professor of Practice of International Politics at the Fletcher School of Law and Diplomacy, Tufts University.

reported conflicts in central Africa, even the most cursory glance at the news headlines reveals a striking lack of order and justice in the world to-day.[1]

Against this backdrop, we must conclude that Global Governance, "a term coined two decades ago to connote hope for effective responses to global problems through collaborative international action, today finds itself in crisis".[2] This crisis puts a particular strain on our trust in the international rule of law and the relevance of international legal institutions. Certainly, criticisms of the lack of enforcement of international obligations and the limited jurisdiction of international courts and tribunals are not new. The observation that "[a]lmost all nations observe almost all principles of international law and almost all of their obligations almost all the time"[3] has consistently been contrasted with the criticism of the "limits of international law",[4] especially during periods of crisis and high stakes in international diplomacy. It follows from this that, in times of multiple crises, times in which the effectiveness of global governance is pressured from multiple angles, the international rule of law is also being undermined in several respects. The various crises mentioned above question our faith in the United Nations' ('UN') system of collective security as framed by the UN Charter; they shatter the idea of a commitment to basic human rights as stipulated in numerous international treaties, while impunity prevails as arrest warrants of the International Criminal Court are being openly flouted by states that have ratified the Rome Statute.[5]

Hence, the quest for order and justice has resonance for both the credibility of contemporary international politics and international law in the century. With an eye to fostering a global rule of law culture, including

---

[1] Note in this regard also that, following steady declines since the end of the Cold War, global indices of armed conflict and violence started to rise again during the past eight years, according to the Institute for Economics and Peace, *Global Peace Index 2015: Measuring Peace, Its Causes and Its Economic Value*, 2014, p. 46.

[2] Commission on Global Security, Justice and Governance, *Confronting the Crisis of Global Governance*, The Hague Institute for Global Justice and the Stimson Center, The Hague, 2015, p. 2.

[3] Louis Henkin, *How Nations Behave*, Columbia University Press, New York, 1979, p. 47.

[4] Eric A. Posner and Jack L. Goldsmith, *The Limits of International Law*, Oxford University Press, New York, 2006.

[5] Joe Sandler Clarke, "South Africa's failure to arrest Omar al-Bashir 'is betrayal of Mandela's ideals'", in *The Guardian*, 24 June 2015.

buttressing viable institutions, the balanced pursuit of both needs to form an integral part of any strategy to reform global governance as it currently stands. Exploring what this might look like, this chapter first discusses the intertwined relationship between order and justice as a conceptual matter. Subsequently, it turns to its application in the international arena, and finally sets out cornerstone conditions for a just international order.

4.2. An Inextricable Link: A Conceptual Understanding of Order and Justice

What, then, is the relationship between order and justice? Are they indivisible concepts at the heart of successful societies? Perhaps contrary aims, pursued in parallel but intrinsically in tension? Or are they merely the elusive concepts of the rhetorician, coupled together as any two abstract nouns might be? Order and justice are indeed linked together. In the kinds of societies we wish to see flourish, and in a world at peace, giving all its peoples the chance of a decent life, order and justice would be two sides of the same coin. In fact, one can go so far as to say that international order is not possible without justice. But it is equally true that, without order, justice will never be secure. In short, a concern for international order must include a concern for justice, and vice versa.

It is important to stress the interconnectedness of order and justice in the type of world that we *want* to live in, because it is readily apparent that, throughout history, there have been attempts to instil order with little concern for justice, or at least without making justice accessible to all, enabling it to serve the interests of all. Too often, order and justice have been in opposition rather than exercised in tandem. The revolt of oppressed peoples yearning for justice against an order imposed by usurping authorities is at the very heart of many countries' founding narratives. In the Netherlands, for instance, history tells of the Dutch people's struggle for justice against an unjust order arbitrarily imposed by foreign rulers. Another example is that of the United States, whose founding documents proclaimed the right of the governed to cast off an unjust government which did not serve their interests. Per the Declaration of Independence:[6]

---

[6] United States Declaration of Independence, 4 July 1776 (http://www.legal-tools.org/doc/cede06/).

> Governments are instituted amongst Men, deriving their just powers from the consent of the governed. […] [W]henever any Form of Government becomes destructive of these ends, it is the Right of the People to alter or to abolish it, and to institute a new Government, laying its foundation on such principles and organizing its powers in such form, as to them shall seem most likely to affect their Safety and Happiness.

As both the Dutch and the Americans had learnt, colonial powers – like other forms of authority with similar aims – frequently appeal to a higher purpose of order to legitimise their rule. Throughout history, however, such claims have generally proved antithetical to the realisation of justice for those over whom colonial powers held sway. The "just powers" which America's Founding Fathers declared a *sine qua non* of legitimate government, have over the past century been increasingly understood as inescapably linked to national self-determination.

A just international order begins, then, with the independence of peoples. Equally, while only anarchists question the need for some kind of order to protect people against the chaos of conflict, most now agree that this must not be the order promised by autocrats throughout history. Past and present dictatorships have exploited disorder to consolidate their power, and used the fear of disorder to justify their rule. But when authority is exercised *solely* to preserve order – invoked for its own sake, and not as a means to an end – it is almost invariably exercised in an arbitrary way, and can even take the form of totalitarian terror. The history of Europe in the twentieth century provides all too many eloquent examples. Consequently, we must understand the legal environment – the rule of law both within and among states – not in 'thin' terms, that is, as simply following rules regardless of their origins and usefulness. Instead, justice in any meaningful sense requires what scholars call a 'thick' conception of the rule of law,[7] with accountable, effective institutions and robust mechanisms for the protection of human rights.

The scholarship and practice of the past few decades have helped us to understand that secure states do not necessarily equate to secure peoples. The notion of 'human security', which suggests that poverty and inequity

---

[7] See further on this distinction Brian Z. Tamanaha, "A Concise Guide to the Rule of Law", in Gianluggi Palombella and Neil Walker (eds.), *Relocating the Rule of Law*, Hart Publishing, 2009.

are the enemies of secure communities just as much as inter-state violence,[8] has made it harder for governments to justify internal repression by invoking the need to guard against external threats. In this context, it was Kofi Annan who spoke of "two concepts of sovereignty" – state sovereignty and individual sovereignty.[9] This radical notion is the cornerstone of the pursuit of a new order which guards against conflict, and in so doing puts the security of the world's peoples – and not just the states in which they live – front and centre. If a just international order begins with states, then it cannot end there; rather, a truly just order must be founded on self-determination not only for states, but more importantly for their citizens.

Order, I would argue, is principally a means to *facilitate* justice. Order *alone* is too often the aspiration of the tyrant. And a *just* order recognises the imperative of human dignity and directs the resources of authority towards its pursuit.

4.3. International Order and Justice

Going beyond the relationship between order and justice within the confines of a given community, most often understood as the nation-state, the world is faced with collective action problems concerning climate change, illicit financial flows and pandemic health emergencies – challenges that Kofi Annan used to call "problems without passports".[10] In the light of such challenges, it becomes clear that the need for justice is not limited to the existence of 193 justly governed states, but extends also to a more effective *international* order, similarly informed by principles of justice. In contemporary philosophy, this insight is the basis for claims to apply John Rawls's seminal theory of justice beyond the confines of the state and develop a notion of 'global justice'.[11]

---

[8] The concept was introduced in: United Nations Development Programme, *Human Development Report 1994*, Oxford University Press, Oxford, 1994, pp. 22–33. It identifies six dimensions: economic, food, health, political, environmental, personal and community security.

[9] Kofi Annan, "Two Concepts of Sovereignty", in *The Economist*, 16 September 1999.

[10] Kofi Annan, "Problems without Passports", in *Foreign Policy*, 9 November 2009.

[11] See, most notably, Charles Beitz, *Political Theory and International Relations*, Princeton University Press, Princeton, 1999; Thomas Pogge, *Realizing Rawls*, Cornell University Press, Ithaca, 1989. See further Darrel Moellendorf and Thomas Pogge (eds.), *Global Justice: Seminal Essays*, Paragon House Publishers, Saint Paul, 2008; and William Durch, Joris Larik and Richard Ponzio, *The Intersection of Security and Justice in Global Governance:*

In the search for better global governance, the domestic analogy is helpful. Just as there have always been those who justify arbitrary rule under the banner of order *within* states, there have been initiatives to reduce chaos and disorder internationally which have shown little concern for the rights and aspirations of individuals, or indeed of smaller states.

The year 2015 marks the two hundredth anniversary of the most famous of such efforts, the Congress of Vienna, known as the Concert of Europe. The Concert was, at its core, an early attempt at international organisation driven by a preoccupation with order. In reaction to the revolutionary convulsions which had emanated from France, and which Napoleon had brought in tow with his conquering armies, the powers of the Concert attempted to restore predictability to international relations.

The Concert, while exhibiting nascent European interest in collective security and external intervention to uphold its guiding principles, differed critically from today's international organisations precisely because of its single-minded focus on order. It was, as the historian of global governance Mark Mazower has written, imbued with "a deeply conservative sense of mission", which was based "on respect for kings and hierarchy" and "prioritized order over equality, stability over justice".[12]

What relevance does a long defunct arrangement such as the Concert of Europe have for our modern understanding of international politics? Its relevance, I would suggest, remains considerable. As Henry Kissinger, who dedicated his doctoral thesis to the Concert, appreciated, this particular form of international order represented both an attempt to innovate international affairs and – of no less interest to Kissinger – a clear attempt to bind an outlying state to the rules of the international game.[13] For Metternich and Castlereagh, the target was France. For Kissinger, it was Soviet Russia. And as geo-political power shifts dramatically in the opening decades of the twenty-first century, attempts to bind rising states such as the BRICS as well as increasingly powerful non-state actors to the preferred international

---

A Conceptual Framework, Background Paper for the Commission on Global Security, Justice and Governance, The Hague Institute for Global Justice, 2015.

[12] Mark Mazower, *Governing the World: The History of an Idea*, Penguin Books, New York, 2013, p. 5.

[13] Published and still available: Henry Kissinger, *A World Restored: Metternich, Castlereagh and the Problems of Peace, 1812-22*, Echo Point Books and Media, 2013.

order of established powers are becoming an increasingly central feature of global affairs.

The Concert was a kind of prototype of such efforts, which replicate internationally the attempt to instil domestic order without justice. This domestic analogy is of a certain use in conceptualising the challenge the world faces, but the task of fostering a just *international* order is significantly more complex. Although the issues which concern our everyday lives are increasingly international in nature, we still operate in a world of nation-states. And though there are mechanisms for those states to co-operate, to deal with common challenges, and even – in the case of the European Union – to pool their power, the prospect of effective global governance still remains a distant one.

Political scientists – more particularly, Realist scholars – tend to see the international sphere as one characterised by anarchy. Without a sovereign, there is little chance of order. And without order, there is no chance of justice. This conceptual understanding of an anarchic world seems echoed in practice by devastating conflicts, failure to make tangible progress on international climate change negotiations, and our inability to agree on common standards to harness the power of the digital era, while leaving the global economy at the mercy of recurrent shocks.

How then do we bring about a just international order which alone can deal with these seemingly intractable global challenges and deliver both peace and prosperity to the world's people? Even in a world of nation-states, and even within an international political system that eschews the Hobbesian 'Leviathan' of world government, more effective co-operation is possible. The contrast between that incipient international organisation, the Concert of Europe, and today's universal multilateral body, the UN, is telling. Whereas the Concert sought to preserve the security of its Member States, including by reacting harshly to expressions of national self-determination, the UN has the declared aim not only to "save succeeding generations from the scourge of war", but also to "reaffirm faith in fundamental human rights" and to "establish conditions under which justice [...] and international law can be maintained".[14]

---

[14] Charter of the United Nations, 26 June 1945, Preamble (http://www.legal-tools.org/doc/6b3cd5/).

Respect for international law, while an important aspect of the global rule of law as *lex lata*, would not be sufficient by itself to establish global justice. However, international law, understood as a legal order which is constantly evolving – including through the authoritative pronouncement of international courts and tribunals – to meet the demands of our age, constitutes a necessary condition for global justice. This idea finds expression in the UN Charter, which stresses the determination of its Member States "to establish conditions under which justice and respect for the obligations arising from treaties and other sources of international law can be maintained".[15] This determination goes hand in hand with the commitment of the – then new – world organisation to promote development (at that time called "social progress and better standards of life in larger freedom")[16] and fundamental human rights, as well as peace. In doing so, the drafters of the UN Charter demonstrated how far international relations had developed in the century since the Concert fell apart. The League of Nations established at the end of the First World War was an important attempt "to achieve international peace and security" and "to promote international cooperation", which were its two main functions.[17] These functions were expected to be complementary, although the former was viewed as the more pressing.

Inspired by this progress, and by what we have achieved in the nearly 70 years *since* the UN Charter was promulgated, a just international order can be seen as a real possibility. What is critical, however, is the marriage of the two core concepts of order and justice. Without order, the world will continue to suffer from deadly conflict, with devastating effects for both lives and livelihoods; without justice, peace will be short-lived, and the gains of development will be felt only by some of the world's people – often only by those in whose hands power has long been concentrated, and perhaps not for long even by them, since such skewed and acquisitive development will not be sustainable. Hence, a just international order is the lodestar for any strategy for global governance reform, as well as for the operation of the principal international bodies, be they more concerned with maintaining order (such as the UN Security Council) or justice (the

---

[15] *Ibid.*

[16] *Ibid.*

[17] Covenant of the League of Nations, 28 June 1919, Preamble (http://www.legal-tools.org/doc/a64206/).

International Court of Justice or the International Criminal Court, among others).

4.4. Conditions for a Just International Order

There are three essential criteria which must be met so as to put order and justice in a mutually-reinforcing relationship. Firstly, there must be peace, based on respect for the liberties and aspirations of all the world's peoples. The designs for world order which are not based accordingly, whether dreamt up by ideologues or hammered out at the conference tables of cynical statesmen, will lack both legitimacy and longevity. With that essential caveat accepted, it nevertheless remains central to the pursuit of a just international order that peace, in its narrowest sense, must obtain. By its narrowest, 'negative' sense, I mean the absence of violence, or the threat of violence,[18] for in conflict nothing else is possible: no development, no rule of law, no hope of realising the potential inherent in every human being. Hence, a Security Council that delivers effectively on its mandate, which is "the maintenance of international peace and security",[19] remains an essential component of both order and justice in the world.

However, a just international order requires more than peace alone. Hence, secondly, there must be the opportunity for the just representation of individual and collective interests. This encompasses much more than the presentation of particular interests in international litigation. At the local and domestic level, it can mean participation in civic affairs through representative democracy, though no single model should be held up as the standard which all countries ought to replicate. At the international level, representation means the ability of all states to participate in international decision-making processes, for their voices to be heard, and for disputes to be managed predictably and equitably. Resolving disputes peacefully can be achieved in many ways, of which judicial recourse is but one option. From this point of view, international legal institutions play an important

---

[18] See, seminally, on the distinction between 'negative' and 'positive' peace: Johan Galtung, "Violence, Peace and Peace Research", in *Journal of Peace Research*, 1969, vol. 6, no. 3, p. 167.

[19] Charter of the United Nations, see *supra* note 14, Article 24(1). In this regard, it should also be recalled that the Security Council, according to the Charter, may be called upon to "make recommendations or decide upon measures to be taken to give effect" to the judgments of the International Court of Justice.

role beyond the adjudication of particular cases covered by their respective jurisdiction. They contribute to the progressive development of international law, amongst others by clarifying principles that guide future behaviour. This is often an under-appreciated aspect of the work of the International Court of Justice and the International Criminal Court, and an essential contribution to the larger picture of constructing an international order based on justice. This, it should be added, will also be the enduring legacy of the Yugoslavia and Rwanda tribunals. Although the institutions have recently ended their work, their contributions to the development of international humanitarian law will have a lasting effect on international law for decades to come.[20]

Finally, more than the mere absence of violence and the chance for all peoples to air their grievances and assert their interests, a just international order requires the creation of genuine opportunities for the development of states, communities, and individuals, bringing with it the prospect of equitable and sustainable development. Societies exhibiting this kind of 'positive peace', in which the rule of law ensures equal access to resources and checks the risk of corruption, are those most likely to flourish and to maintain peace with their neighbours as well as within their borders. Such positive peace cannot be brought about either by the Security Council or international courts – although they retain a crucial role in establishing the conditions under which other actors can build positive peace in an environment that is marked by both security and legal certainty. The most recent expression of what positive peace means in the twenty-first century are the Sustainable Development Goals adopted in 2015, which succeed the Millennium Development Goals. As becomes readily apparent from their content, goals such as ending extreme poverty, world hunger and bringing about gender equality, cannot be achieved by Security Council Resolutions or judgments of the International Court of Justice. They require the sustained and concerted effort of the international community as a whole,

---

[20] See Larissa van den Herik, "The Contribution of the Rwanda Tribunal to the Development of International Law", in *Developments in International Law*, 2005, vol. 53; and Bert Swart, Alexander Zahar and Göran Sluiter (eds.), *The Legacy of the International Criminal Tribunal for the Former Yugoslavia*, Oxford University Press, New York, 2011.

including civil society, the private sector and states from both the Global North and South, to stand a chance at being met.[21]

These three conditions – peace, representation, and opportunity – are informed by the principles of equality, whether of sovereign states or of individuals, and of liberty. These pillars of a just international order turn old notions of order on their head by demonstrating that order flows *from* freedom, rather than requiring its curtailment. It is a vision which should be at the heart of contemporary international affairs and of the many global actors' strategies for governance reform.

4.5.   The Role of the UN and the Need for Better Global Governance

The UN has a critical role to play in promoting a just international order – a role that is multi-faceted and incorporates all aspects of the three conditions of just order discussed above.[22] It is the UN, through the Security Council, that has the primary responsibility for maintaining international peace and security, and in so doing, preventing the eruption of deadly conflict which undermines both order and justice. It is the UN, furthermore, that provides all states with a representative forum, and through its institutional machinery can ensure that their interests are taken into account. And it is the UN, finally, which provides *normative leadership*, by advancing aims such as human rights, gender equality and sustainable development, through the work of its agencies, funds and programmes, the policies agreed on by its members, and the public pronouncements of its leaders.[23] This includes judicial institutions – not least the International Court of Justice as the "principal judicial organ of the United Nations", known by many also as the 'World Court' – but also many other, non-judicial actors, which all play an important part in the UN's normative leadership. In this context, last but not least, Secretary-General Ban Ki-moon launched the Human Rights Up Front Initiative in 2013, which enlists the entire UN system in

---

[21] See also, on the engagement of a broad range of non-state actors in conflict prevention and sustainable peacebuilding: The Hague Institute for Global Justice, *The Hague Approach Six Principles for Achieving Sustainable Peace in Post-Conflict Situations*, 2013.

[22] See also Abiodun Williams, "John Holmes Memorial Lecture", in *Global Governance: A Review of Multilateralism and International Organizations*, 2016, vol. 22, pp. 27–39.

[23] The multi-dimensional nature of the UN thus goes beyond the widening scope of relevant actors, as postulated in Thomas Weiss, Tatiana Carayannis and Richard Jolly, "The 'Third' United Nations", in *Global Governance: A Review of Multilateralism and International Organizations*, 2009, vol. 15, p. 123.

the promotion and protecting of human rights, and not merely courts, treaty-bodies or specific organs such as the Human Rights Council.

However, in order to be able to play that unique role, the UN is in serious need of reform. The Security Council – which represents the political realities of 1945 – fails the test of representation on which a just international order depends. This is gradually eroding its legitimacy, and thereby limiting its effectiveness in fulfilling its mandate to maintain international peace and security. Similar observations can be made about the world's foremost justice institutions. To date, only about a third of the world's countries have recognised the compulsory jurisdiction of the International Court of Justice, which limits the Court's relevance and legitimacy in addressing some of the most pressing legal questions of our time in a judicially authoritative manner. Moreover, the International Criminal Court remains outside the UN system altogether, and lacks the backing of major powers including three of the five permanent members of the Security Council.

Acknowledging the realities, one must admit that, even if reformed, the UN will still have its limits, and will remain an imperfect institution. There are sound reasons for this. As the great American statesman, Ralph Bunche, remarked when accepting the Nobel Peace Prize:[24]

> [T]he United Nations itself is but a cross section of the world's peoples. It reflects, therefore, the typical fears, suspicions, and prejudices which bedevil human relations throughout the world.

These limits were acknowledged even by one of the Organization's foremost leaders, Dag Hammarskjöld, who famously remarked that the body had not been "created to take mankind to heaven, but to save humanity from hell".[25] Hammarskjöld, however, combined a realistic humility about the UN's purposes with bold and visionary leadership, thereby maximising the Organization's potential where it *did* have a special role to play. His tenure as Secretary-General should remind us that realism about the UN's deficiencies does not entail fatalism about the opportunities it presents.

---

[24] Ralph Bunche, *Some Reflections on Peace in Our Time*, Nobel Lecture, 11 December 1950, available on the web site of the Nobel Committee.

[25] As quoted, for instance, in Thomas Weiss, *Global Governance: Why? What? Whither?*, Polity Press, Cambridge, 2013, p. 2.

We should also remember that the UN has proved, time and again, that with inspired leaders who are willing to act as 'norm entrepreneurs', both within the Secretariat and among Member States, path-breaking change is indeed possible. A formidable example for this is the emerging norm of the Responsibility to Protect, which derives from the understanding that peoples are sovereign, rather than states, and that violations of the most fundamental human rights demand a response – if not from their own governments, then from the international community.[26] This understanding is an essential component of a just international order.

The Responsibility to Protect has developed from the recognition that, in several instances – especially in Rwanda and Bosnia – the UN manifestly failed in its duty to protect civilians. Other innovations, including more robust peace-keeping mandates, a greater emphasis on protection of civilians and a more effective international human rights architecture, stem from the same approach which Hammarskjöld modelled and which Kofi Annan inherited: reflection on the UN's deficiencies, acknowledgement of the limits of its influence, and bold leadership where action is indeed possible.

The reforms which the UN requires today will depend on wider recognition of the conditions of a just international order. Kofi Annan's understanding of order with justice provides encouragement for those who believe both that the inherent dignity of the individual should guide world affairs, and that international institutions offer a path for its realisation. His own landmark report, *In Larger Freedom,* underscored this belief. According to the Report, the "protection and promotion of the universal values of the rule of law, human rights and democracy are ends in themselves".[27] Consequently, they "are also essential for a world of justice, opportunity and stability",[28] and no "security agenda and no drive for development will be successful unless they are based on the sure foundation of respect for

---

[26] See seminally Gareth Evans *et al., The Responsibility to Protect: The Report of the International Commission on Intervention and State Sovereignty*, IDRC Books, Ottawa, 2001.

[27] United Nations General Assembly, *In larger freedom: towards development, security and human rights for all*, Report of the Secretary-General, UN Doc. A/59/2005, 21 March 2005, p. 34 (http://www.legal-tools.org/doc/5739f5/).

[28] *Ibid.*

human dignity".[29] In other words, order, according to Annan, is founded on justice.

4.6. Conclusion

In this chapter, I have sought to elaborate on the intricate relationship between order and justice in Global Governance, the difficulties of achieving both in the current international environment marked by a multitude of parallel and interrelated crises, and the crucial role of the UN in this regard. At the outset, it was noted that the current crisis of Global Governance does not only have the immediate effect of undermining order and security in many places in the world, but furthermore puts into question our faith in the international rule of law and the relevance of international legal institutions. Without international institutions capable of maintaining order under the vanguard of the UN Security Council, achieving international justice becomes an illusion. At the same time, in order to be sustainable, to incorporate and strengthen at the global level the separation of powers, and systems of checks and balances – known as principles of good governance in the domestic sphere – judicial bodies are needed to interpret and apply the law, and to develop it further in an authoritative manner. I posited three conditions for a just international order: peace, representation, and opportunity. Regarding the latter two, it was noted that we have to look further than international courts or the Security Council, and include all states as well as important non-state actors. While the Council plays an important role in bringing about safety, stability and predictability as necessary background conditions for positive peace, many other actors, including the UN system as a whole, are called upon to produce what the Charter calls "life in larger freedom" on a global scale.

Although the challenges that the world faces today are serious, and although there will always be those attracted by an order which concentrates power in the hands of the few not the many, we can be optimistic about the possibility of a just order for our world, because of what has been achieved by the pioneers of justice, both within states and on the international stage, and because the tools for a just international order are at our disposal. What is required is merely the will to put them to work. If we make it our common endeavour, order with justice can be the hallmark of

---

[29] *Ibid.*

international life in the decades to come. Right now, it is a noble aspiration: our task is to make it a reality.

5

Changes in the Russian Legal Environment: Signs of Preparation for 'Cold War II'

Ekaterina A. Mishina*

5.1. Introduction

The events of 2014 surrounding Ukraine clearly demonstrated that Western policy-makers were not prepared to devise a timely and nuanced response to the sudden escalation of geo-political ambitions in the Kremlin power circle. Numerous political analysts pointed out that this lack of preparation was largely due to incomplete understanding of intentions and goals of the Russian political bloc determined to start 'Cold War II'. At the same time, there were clear signals that Russia was openly departing from the traditions of democracy and fundamental principles of the rule of law, separation of powers and supremacy of human rights. These signals included:

- rampant escalation of the Soviet imperial ambitions that remained latent in the 1990s and 2000s;
- further increase of xenophobia and setting up of aggressive nationalist groups, as demonstrated by the Anti-Maidan;
- continuous repression of political opponents, where the killing of Boris Nemtsov, a former Deputy Prime-Minister of Russia and one of the leaders of the Russian opposition movement, serves as the most obvious example;
- witch-hunts and prosecution of dissent; and
- re-instatement of certain typical characteristics of the Soviet regime including:
    - censorship;
    - semi-official restrictions of freedom of movement;

---

* **Ekaterina A. Mishina**, Ph.D., Independent Scholar. She was Visiting Professor at the University of Michigan in 2012–2016, and Associate Professor at the Law Faculty, National Research University Higher School of Economics (HSE University), in 2005–2014.

- politicisation of the system of secondary and higher education;
- aggressive official propaganda;
- anti-Semitism, as seen with the Fifth Jewish Column;
- the concept of 'people's enemy'; and
- "moral values of the Russian society" as opposed to the universally recognised principles of rule of law, supremacy of human rights and separation of powers.

5.2. Bills Exemplifying Changes in Russian Politics

In Russia, a legislative draft never expires once it is introduced in the Parliament. Accordingly, it is possible to retrieve and analyse the vast accumulation of recent legislative proposals aimed at self-isolation and political repression in Russia. Many of these now-dormant bills can be quickly signed into law when politically convenient. Any significant event on the geo-political front can, in principle, serve as a trigger for co-ordinated reaction on the part of Russian legislators. If this happens, the world might be surprised to see Russia's almost instantaneous regress towards totalitarian, reactionary state whose hold on power is based on violence, overt violation of human rights and political repression under legalistic cover. Below are several examples of bills that clearly indicate the anti-Western 'back to the USSR' trend in contemporary Russian politics.

In the Fall of 2014, the bill targeting removal of the ban on state ideology from the Russian Constitution was submitted to the State Duma.[1] On 3 December 2014, the bill addressing the so-called 'aggressor states',[2] which may seriously impede economic ties with Russia, made its way to the lower house of the Russian Parliament. The implications of the proposed cleansing of foreign elements from the Russian economy (including foreign auditing companies) will automatically result in a loss of foreign investors' confidence in Russian companies. As another consequence, the market for such companies' shares will inevitably collapse. The possible consequences of the expulsion of foreign law firms will be extremely severe for Russian business, and particularly for those companies whose

---

[1] Juliana Demesheva, "State Ideology May Return to Russia", in *Institute of Modern Russia*, 28 October 2014.

[2] Ekaterina A. Mishina, "The State Duma Wants to Protect Russia from Foreigners", in *Institute of Modern Russia*, 17 December 2014.

relations with foreign counterparts are regulated not by Russian laws, but by those of some other country. On 12 March 2015, a bill envisaging limitation of attendance of rallies, demonstrations, street processions and pickets by foreign citizens and stateless persons was officially introduced to the State Duma.[3] The draft suggests limiting participation of foreigners and stateless persons in Russian political events "in order to prevent provocations". Amendments envisaging payment of work pensions to the denouncers of the operative/investigative agencies were signed into law on 29 June 2015.[4]

In early December 2015, a bill envisaging criminalisation of the transfer of consumer goods for amounts over 250,000 roubles (approximately USD 3,500) was placed on the Russian government web site for public discussion. The drafters suggested making the transfer of such consumer goods over the customs border of the Eurasian Economic Union illegal and punishable by a fine (300,000–1,000,000 roubles) or five years' imprisonment. The maximum imprisonment term would be raised to 12 years if committed by an organised crime group. Notably, under the 1960 Criminal Code of the Russian Soviet Federative Socialist Republic, smuggling, or illegal transfer of goods or other valuables over the state border of the Union of Soviet Socialist Republics was punishable by up to 10 years of deprivation of freedom with confiscation of property. Smuggling was decriminalised in December 2011 in the time of the so-called 'Medvedev's thaw'. Now, the Russian Federation's Criminal Code has been amended to include four new articles:[5]

- Article 200.1 on illegal transfer of cash and/or monetary instruments over the customs border of the Eurasian Economic Union committed on a large scale;

---

[3]   ГАРАНТ.РУ, "Иностранцам могут ограничить участие в публичных мероприятиях на территории России" [Foreigners can limit their participation in public events on the territory of Russia], 12 March 2015.

[4]   RGRU, "Федеральный закон от 29 июня 2015 г. N 173-ФЗ 'О внесении изменений в отдельные законодательные акты Российской Федерации в части пенсионного обеспечения некоторых категорий граждан'" [Federal Law No. 173-FZ of June 29, 2015, 'On Amending Certain Legislative Acts of the Russian Federation Regarding Pension Provision for Certain Categories of Citizens'], Federal Issue No. 6715 (144), 3 July 2015.

[5]   Criminal Code of the Russian Federation, N 63-FZ, 13 June 1996, as amended on 23 and 25 April 2013 (http://www.legal-tools.org/doc/31ddce/).

- Article 200.2 on smuggling of alcohol and/or tobacco goods over the customs border of the Customs Union committed on a large scale;
- Article 226.1 on illegal trafficking of hazardous substances, specific goods, and cultural property; and
- Article 229.1 on illegal trafficking of narcotic drugs, psychotropic substances and their precursors and analogues.

According to the Federal Customs Service of Russia,[6] 239 criminal cases were opened pursuant to Article 226.1, and 323 criminal cases were opened under Article 229.1.

Various pieces of Russian legislation adopted in 2012–2015, as well as certain rulings of the Russian Constitutional Court, reveal the same dangerous trend. In July 2012, amendments to the Russian Federation's Federal Law on Noncommercial Organisations and Law on Public Associations introduced the concept of a 'foreign agent'. According to the new Article 2(6) of the Federal Law on non-governmental organisations ('NGOs'), a 'foreign agent' is now any Russian NGO receiving "cash and other property from foreign governments and their public authorities, international and foreign organisations, foreign citizens, stateless persons or persons authorised by them, and (or) from Russian legal entities receiving cash and other property from foreign sources," and involved "in political activities on the territory of the Russian Federation, including for the benefit of foreign sources". These amendments created a legal framework for official persecution of Russian NGOs which the regime deems undesirable.

In April 2014, the Russian Constitutional Court ruled that these amendments were constitutional and expanded the definition of 'political activities' to include "intention to participate in political activities on the territory of the Russian Federation". Evidence of such intentions, according to the Constitutional Court, can be found in an NGO's official documents, or the public speeches of its leaders or officials containing "calls to adopt, amend, or repeal certain government decisions, notices of meetings, rallies, demonstrations, marches and pickets submitted by the non-profit organisation to the executive authority of a subject of the Russian Federation or to

---

[6] Russian Federal Customs Service, "Results of law enforcement activity of the Federal Customs Service of Russia in H1, 2014", 13 May 2018, available on the web site of the Federal Customs Service.

a local authority, drafting and launching of legislative initiatives, as well as other manifestations of social activity, that are objective evidence of its intention to engage in organisation and conduct of political campaigns in order to influence decision-making by public authorities and their public policies". Noting the various forms of political action, the Constitutional Court included in this category "public appeals to public authorities, disseminating [...] assessments of decisions taken by public authorities and their policies, as well as other activities, an exhaustive list of which cannot be legislatively established". The last part of the sentence is key, as it establishes an open-ended definition of what constitutes 'political action' – one that is vague and dimensionless. Thus, the Ministry of Justice, in its sole discretion, and referring to the ruling of the Constitutional Court, may qualify virtually any action by an NGO (including the organisation of an event) as 'political action', if it detects an intent "to influence, directly or through the formation of public opinion, decisions by public authorities and their public policies, and aimed at getting wide publicity and getting the attention of the state apparatus and (or) civil society".

As of 16 December 2015, 108 Russian NGOs were labelled 'foreign agents'.[7] This list includes such famous organisations as the Glasnost Defense Foundation (one of the oldest Russian NGOs, created in 1991, which monitors violations of the rights of journalists and media outlets on the territory of Russia and provides legal aid to journalists and representatives of mass media), Memorial (a human rights group) and the Dynasty Foundation (the first private non-profit foundation to sponsor science and education in modern Russia, with the main objective of finding and supporting talented people and their ideas and projects in the fields of natural and social sciences. The priority activities of the foundation were to develop fundamental science and education in Russia, facilitate scientific research in the country, and to promote science and education). After being blacklisted as a 'foreign agent', the Dynasty Foundation discontinued its operations on 31 October 2015.

In November 2012, amendments to the Russian Criminal Code extensively broadened the definition of 'high treason'. In its initial wording,

---

[7]   Russian Ministry of Justice, "Сведения реестра НКО, выполняющих функции иностранного агента" [Information of the register of NGOs performing the functions of a foreign agent], available on the website of the Ministry of Justice.

Article 275 defined 'high treason' as "espionage, transfer of a state secret or any provision of assistance to a foreign government, foreign organisation or their representatives in their conduct of hostile actions to the detriment of the external security of the Russian Federation, committed by a citizen of the Russian Federation". As amended, Article 275 defines 'high treason' as an act that:[8]

> is committed by a citizen of the Russian Federation, acts of espionage, disclosure to a foreign state, an international or foreign organisation, or their representatives of information constituting a state secret that has been entrusted or has become known to that person through service, work, study or in other cases determined by the legislation of the Russian Federation, or any financial, material and technical, consultative or other assistance to a foreign state, an international or foreign organisation, or their representatives in activities against the security of the Russian Federation.

The following are the most dangerous pitfalls of this new wording:

- The phrase "hostile actions to the detriment of the external security of the Russian Federation" is replaced by the ambiguous phrase "activities against the security of the Russian Federation". The omission of the word "hostile" essentially makes this concept ambiguous.
- The new definition covers not only external but also internal security. A clear and detailed definition of both concepts is absent from the Criminal Code.
- The ambiguity of the wording "financial, material and technical, consultative or other assistance to a foreign state, an international or foreign organisation, or their representatives in activities against the security of the Russian Federation" makes the article applicable to almost any activity.
- International organisations are identified as potential recipients of information constituting state secrets, as well as of the above-mentioned types of assistance. A list of such recipients was intentionally made open-ended, so it can include any international organisation by default.

---

[8]   Criminal Code of the Russian Federation, see *supra* note 5.

- The vagueness of this statutory provision makes it impossible for citizens to properly abide by it, a violation of one of the fundamental conditions of the rule of law.
- The ambiguity creates unlimited possibilities for arbitrary interpretation and selective application. Pursuant to Article 275, a criminal case for 'high treason' can be initiated against any citizen of the Russian Federation who provides someone almost any information or commits almost any action.

The list of people convicted of high treason includes a Ukrainian filmmaker Oleg Sentzov (who received 20 years' imprisonment), Professor Evgeny Afanasyev (who received 12.5 years' imprisonment and died in prison in April 2015), Professor Svyatoslav Bobyshev (who received 12 years' imprisonment), four Russian Navy servicemen and others. In June 2013, after numerous attempts to re-criminalise sodomy, Russia introduced administrative responsibility for 'gay propaganda'. The infamous new article of Russia's Code of Administrative Offences quickly found its way to the Russian Constitutional Court. In the decision issued on 23 September 2014, the Court ruled Article 6.21 to be constitutional. The legal reasoning of this ruling clearly states that Russia does not support the internationally-recognised notion of anti-discrimination as it contradicts to traditional Russian values. The aim pursued by federal law-makers in establishing this norm was to protect children from information that could push them to non-traditional sexual relations, the adherence to which hinders the development of family relations as they are traditionally understood in Russia, and as they are manifested in the Constitution of the Russian Federation.[9]

December 2013 saw criminalisation of "[p]ublic calls for acts directed at violation of territorial integrity of Russia", which preceded annexation of Crimea. In May 2014, Russian Criminal Code was amended with a new article imposing criminal responsibility for rehabilitation of Nazism.

---

[9] RGRU, "Постановление Конституционного Суда Российской Федерации от 23 сентября 2014 г. N 24-П город Санкт-Петербург 'по делу о проверке конституционности части 1 статьи 6.21 Кодекса Российской Федерации об административных правонарушениях в связи с жалобой граждан Н.А. Алексеева, Я.Н. Евтушенко и Д.А. Исакова'" [Resolution of the Constitutional Court of the Russian Federation No. 24-P of September 23, 2014, the City of St. Petersburg 'in the case on the verification of the constitutionality of part 1 of Article 6.21 of the Code of Administrative Offences of the Russian Federation in connection with the complaint of citizens N.A. Alekseeva, J.N. Evtushenko and D.A. Isakova'], Federal Issue No. 6498 (226), 3 October 2014.

The definition of this crime includes a dangerous provision that criminalises "public dissemination of false information on the role and activities of the USSR during WWII". In August 2014, amendments to the Russian legislation introduced the obligation on Russian citizens who have a second nationality or a residence permit in a different country to notify the Federal Migration Service in writing. These changes include criminalisation of failure to report second citizenship or a residence permit – the Criminal Code was amended with Article 330.2, which concerns the "Failure to Comply with the Obligation to Notify of the Citizenship (Nationality) of a Foreign State or a Residence Permit or other Document Confirming the right to live permanently in a foreign state".[10]

This violation was made punishable by a fine of up to 200,000 roubles, or up to an amount equal to the offender's annual income or by compulsory labour for a term of up to 400 hours. Apparently, the drafters of these amendments neglected to acquaint themselves with the criminal law. Otherwise, they would have known that the criminalisation of acts is based on a number of qualifying characteristics, such as culpability, punishability, and public danger, as set out in Article 14 of the Criminal Code. Article 14(2) expressly provides that "an action [inaction] is not considered a crime, although it can formally contain any characteristics of an offense under this Code, but because [such an action] does not represent any public danger due to its insignificance". Public danger is one criterion used in defining a crime that constitutes a socially dangerous act that harms or threatens to harm the individual, society, or the state. The social danger that results from a Russian citizen's failure to inform the relevant authorities about his or her possession of another state's citizenship or residence permit was never made clear.

The problem of dual citizenship and the desire to criminalise it has preoccupied domestic legislators for a long time. In 2000, Alexei Mitrofanov, a member of the Russian Parliament, prepared and submitted a draft law to the State Duma, in which he proposed criminalising the acquisition of another state's citizenship by a Russian Federation citizen. Shortly thereafter, he proposed adding the following language to Article 136 of the Criminal Code:

---

[10] Criminal Code of the Russian Federation, see *supra* note 5.

> Acquisition by a person of the nationality of another state
> while temporarily staying or residing outside the Russian Fed-
> eration, while retaining the citizenship of the Russian Federa-
> tion, shall be illegal.

Upon closer examination, this language is not too different from some of
the provisions of the notorious Article 64 of the 1960 Criminal Code of the
Russian Soviet Federative Socialist Republic (upheld by the Russian Constitutional Court on 20 December 1995), which labelled the refusal to return
from abroad or the act of fleeing abroad as treason. It is noteworthy that the
Third State Duma considered this bill in the first reading in October 2002
and responded sensibly. The Law Committee said that the bill contradicted
the provisions of Article 6 of the Constitution, noting that it is difficult to
define the acquisition of another country's citizenship as a socially dangerous act. The Legal Department of the State Duma decided that "the proposed project establishing criminal liability for actions aimed at a Russian
citizen's acquisition of the citizenship of another state raises serious objections" and was unacceptable. By the end of 2014, 43 thousand Russian citizens were held administratively liable for violation of Article 19.8.3 of the
Russian Code of Administrative Offences concerning "Violation of the Established Order of Reporting the Citizenship (Nationality) of a Foreign
State or a Residence Permit or other Document Confirming the right to live
permanently in a foreign state".[11] The first criminal case was opened in December 2014.

Acts insulting religious feelings were criminalised in June 2013
shortly after the Pussy Riot case. For organising a so-called "punk prayer"
in Moscow's Christ the Saviour Cathedral in February 2012, Pussy Riot
members were arrested and later sentenced to two years in prison. Despite
individual tastes and attitudes toward the band's performance, Pussy Riot
members should not have been subjected to such harsh legal penalties or
such heavy-handed treatment by law enforcement. If their actions had been
assessed objectively, Pussy Riot members would have been fined 1,000
roubles at most, and this would have been the end of it. The Russian legislation in effect at the time of the violation established the sanction that
should have been applied in such a case for "offense of religious feelings
of believers and/or desecration of items, signs and emblems of religious

---

[11] Russian Code of Administrative Offences, N 195-FZ, 30 December 2001, as amended 23
April 2013, and amended and supplemented effective from 14 May 2013, Article 19.8.3.

reverence".[12] This exactly fits the violation committed by Pussy Riot in Moscow's Christ the Saviour Cathedral, and it has little overlap with 'hooliganism', the violation of which the participants were convicted. In other words, the "punk prayer" was an administrative offence, that is, an unlawful, guilty act that is characterised by a considerably lower degree of public danger than a crime. In this particular case, nevertheless, *who* did it and *how* it was done was more important than *what* was done. This was the incorrect, one-sided and biased approach to evidence taken by Judge Marina Syrova, who stated that the behaviour of the accused in the courtroom should be considered as yet further proof of their guilt – an interpretation that ensured the required result: the members of Pussy Riot were not found guilty of what they actually did, but, according to the best traditions of early Soviet criminal justice, were sentenced on the basis of their categorisation as socially dangerous individuals.

5.3. Other Changes in the Russian Legal Landscape

Russia was making strong efforts to get closer to European traditions and values in the 1990s, due to a considerable extent to the efforts of President Yeltsyn. Russia became a member of the Council of Europe in 1996 and ratified the European Convention on Human Rights ('ECtHR') in March 1998. By doing this, Russia undertook the responsibility of bringing national legislation in conformity with provisions of the Convention. At that time, Russia was serious about this obligation: the initial version of the Russian Code of Criminal Procedure, which was adopted in 2001, serves as the best example.

This approach dramatically changed in the last decade. Talks about potentially not enforcing judgments of the European Court of Human Rights were initiated by the Chief Justice of the Russian Constitutional Court, Valery Zorkin, after the ECtHR ruling of 7 October 2010 on the case of Russian serviceman Konstantin Markin, where the European Convention on Human Rights ('ECHR') found that there had been gender-based discrimination in the exercise of an individual's right to private and family life.[13] The ECtHR's ruling offended Zorkin, and on 29 October 2010, *Rossiyskaya Gazeta,* an official Russian newspaper, published his article

---

[12]   *Ibid.*, Article 5.26(2).

[13]   European Court of Human Rights, *Konstantin Markin v. Russia*, Application No. 30078/06, Judgment, 7 October 2010.

entitled 'The Limits of Compliance'. In that article, Zorkin characterised the ECtHR's decision as a turning point in the relationship between the Constitutional Court and the ECtHR, saying, "For the first time the European Court has questioned a decision of the Constitutional Court of the Russian Federation in tough legal terms". Moreover, Zorkin perceived this ruling as an infringement upon Russia's sovereignty. Several weeks later, speaking on the International Forum on Constitutional Justice, he made the point that, although Russia signed the ECHR, as well as a number of protocols, thus recognising the jurisdiction of the ECtHR and undertaking to be bound by its decisions, "if Russia wishes, it can withdraw from the jurisdiction of the ECtHR". He returned to these issues several times in his other articles usually published in *Rossiyskaya Gazeta*.

On 14 July 2015, the Constitutional Court of Russia issued a decision that embodied the concept of supremacy of the Russian Constitution. The official press release clearly stated that Russia's participation in an international treaty does not imply relinquishment of national sovereignty; thus, neither the ECHR, nor ECtHR legal positions based on the ECHR, can override the supremacy of the Russian Constitution. Their practical implementation in the Russian legal system is possible only on the condition that the Russian Basic Law is recognised as the supreme legal force. The press release further stipulated that the Constitution of the Russian Federation and the ECHR are based on common core values, and conflicts usually do not occur, but may occur if the ECtHR interprets the ECHR in a way that contravenes the Constitution. In such a situation, Russia, by virtue of the supremacy of the Basic Law, will be compelled to withdraw from literal compliance with a decision by the Strasbourg Court.

The decision stipulated that the supremacy of the Constitution can be ensured only by the Constitutional Court, using one of two procedures:

- Reviewing the constitutionality of legislation in which the ECtHR has found flaws. The relevant inquiry must be submitted by a court of general jurisdiction or an arbitration court, which must perform a procedure to review the case on the basis of the ECtHR decision; or
- Interpreting the Constitution at the request of Russia's President or government, once the authorities have determined that a particular ruling by the ECtHR in relation to Russia cannot be enforced without contradicting the Basic Law.

The decision also authorised law-makers to establish, on behalf of the Constitutional Court, a special legal mechanism to ensure the supremacy of the Constitution in the enforcement of ECtHR decisions. This was done in December 2015, when a set of amendments to the 1994 Federal Constitutional Law on the Constitutional Court of Russia empowering the Constitutional Court to decide on the possibility of enforcement of the ECtHR judgments in Russia was approved by the Parliament and signed into law by the Russian President.

In May 2015, the law on foreign 'undesirable organisations' was passed. In July 2015, Russian senators came up with the so-called 'stop-list', which included 12 foreign NGOs (most of them linked with the United States). The Federation Council said then that the activities of these NGOs were aimed at influencing the internal political situation in Russia. Under this draconian law, the National Endowment for Democracy, the McArthur Foundation, the Open Society Foundation, the Open Society Assistance Foundation and the U.S. Russia Foundation for Economic Advancement and the Rule of Law were blacklisted as undesirable organisations in Russian territory.

In 2014, amendments to the Russian Criminal Code introduced a new crime under Article 212.1 concerning "Repeated violation of the established order of organisation or holding an assembly, rally, demonstration, street procession or picketing", with the sanction amounting to up to five years' imprisonment. Under the Code of Administrative Offences, a single or second violation of that kind constitutes an administrative offence punishable by huge fines or up to 30 days of administrative arrest. These provisions were passed on as a follow-up to the 2014 amendments to the law on public assemblies. On 7 December 2015, a peaceful opposition activist Ildar Dadin was found guilty for repeated violations of the established order of conducting meetings, rallies, and street processions. The judge at Moscow's Basmanny Court sentenced Ildar Dadin to three years in jail, despite prosecutors having requested a two-year prison sentence. Another unprecedented development was that Dadin's father testified against his son, though Article 51 of the Russian Constitution clearly states that no one shall be obliged to give incriminating evidence, husband or wife and close relatives.

These legislative developments:

- confirm that Russia is departing from the universal principles of democracy;
- target freedom of speech, freedom of assembly and other constitutional rights;
- reinstate and encourage a hostile perception of foreigners;
- facilitate the creation lists of untrustworthy individuals, national NGOs and foreign organisations;
- bring back certain features of the Soviet way of treating dissent;
- revive the worst traditions of early Soviet criminal law;
- constitute legislative background for further escalation of authoritarianism in Russia and its possible transformation into totalitarianism; and
- signal that Russia is ready for 'Cold War II'.

5.4. Conclusion

I seriously doubt that Russian political leadership will successfully restore the Soviet Union, or its limited version. Similarly, today it is hardly possible to bring the Iron Curtain back. At the same time, there are obvious signs that slowly, but steadily, Russia is dissociating itself from the Western world. Russian politicians, media and the representatives of all three branches of power, with the active participation of the Constitutional Court, repeatedly point out the differences between the European democratic principles and Russian traditional and cultural values. The way Russia currently treats its international obligations brings up serious concerns. Assessing the 2015 amendments to the Federal Constitutional Law on the Constitutional Court of the Russian Federation of 1994, the Venice Commission argued the following:[14]

> [T]he Russian Constitutional Court has been empowered to declare an international decision as "unenforceable", which prevents the execution of that decision in any manner whatsoever in the Russian Federation. This is incompatible with the obligations of the Russian Federation under international law. A possible declaration of unenforceability of a judgment of the European Court of Human Rights violates Article 46 of

---

[14] Council of Europe, Russian Federation on the Amendments to the Constitutional Law on the Constitutional Court of the Russian Federation, Opinion No. 832/2015, CDL-AD(2016)016, 13 June 2016.

the European Convention on Human Rights, which is an une-
quivocal legal obligation and includes the obligation for the
State to abide by the interpretation and the application of the
Convention made by the Court in cases brought against it.

The fact that Russia has legitimised the possibility to violate its obligations
under the ECHR sends disturbing signals to the rest of the world. On 16
November 2016, Russia withdrew its signature of the Statute of the International Criminal Court, signalling that it does not intend to become bound
by its jurisdiction.[15] Such an approach may result in weakening of long-
established international economic and trade ties, worsening of political
contacts with the European and overseas states, and Russia's possible withdrawal from the Council of Europe.

---

[15] Anna Baidakova, "Москва защитилась от Гааги: Россия вышла из-под юрисдикции
Международного уголовного суда, пока там расследуют конфликт на Украине" [Mos-
cow defended from The Hague: Russia withdrew from the jurisdiction of the International
Criminal Court, while they are investigating the conflict in Ukraine], in *Novaya Gazeta*, 18
November 2016.

6

Global Constitutionalism and Brazil:
Between Peripheral Constitutionalism
and Trans-constitutionalism

Marcelo Neves*

6.1. Constitutionalism as a 'Misplaced Idea'

The debate concerning the introduction of constitutional conceptions in Brazil historically concentrated on the divergence between two basic views: one points to a detachment from cultural authenticity through the absorption of foreign elements which deny Brazil's – or the Brazilian Nation's – identity, singularities or peculiarities; the other suggests a deficiency, a flaw in our capacity to implement liberal values, superior in terms of civilisation and to be followed as models. Beyond the sphere of politics and law, the first orientation finds a literary expression in a famous passage by Machado de Assis:[1]

> The real country is good, it reveals the best instincts; but the official country is caricatural and burlesque. [...] There are certain political fortunes in our land that cannot be explained.

The opposing orientation is expressed in a statement by Tobias Barreto, in which he compared the experience of the moderating power, established by the Constitution of 1824, with English parliamentarism:[2]

---

* **Marcelo Neves** is Professor of Public Law at the University of Brasilia Law School.

[1] Joaquim Maria Machado De Assis, "Crônica de 29 de dezembro de 1861 no Diário do Rio de Janeiro" [Chronicle of December 29, 1861 in the Diário do Rio de Janeiro], in *Obras Completas de Machado de Assis* [Complete Works of Machado de Assis], vol. 22, *Crônicas* [Chronicles] no. 1, W.M. Jackson Inc., Rio de Janeiro, 1955, pp. 104–105.

[2] Tobias Barreto, *Estudos de direito* [Law Studies], Bookseller, Campinas, 2000, pp. 375–424, p. 383. However, see p. 417 for Barreto's reservations in his negative assessment of the Brazilian political experience: "It is clear that it is not only the good side, but also the bad side of the English government, indispensable to the conservation and harmony of the whole, that cannot be transmitted to any other country".

> The institutions that are not born of custom, but are an abstract product of reason, cannot stand the trial of experience for very long, and soon find themselves broken before the facts. Indubitably, our government is in such a state. [...] But it is important not to forget that the complicity of the people plays a role in the production of our misfortunes.

These two ways of considering the relationship between "real country" and "official country" or, from the politico-legal point of view, dealing with the presence of liberal ideas and institutions of European origin in Brazil are diverse expressions of a self-understanding which was tentatively called 'misplaced ideas'.[3]

Underlying this debate is the conception that Brazilian society has a particular identity which distinguishes it from European societies. This conception drives the constant search for the peculiarity, singularity or authenticity of Brazil. In this context, the notion of society is linked to the politico-cultural concept of nation-state, involving territoriality itself. 'Nation' as a cultural concept played a decisive role in the romantic tradition of the nineteenth century. The Brazilian nation is presented as a cultural expression of a particular society, whereas the state is understood as a political manifestation of the nation. That notion returns a peculiar semantics and structure akin to the Brazilian society, which would allow its comprehension and explanation. It is in this sense that the label 'interpreters of Brazil'[4] was coined.

I adopt, however, the theoretical supposition that modern society emerges as a world society.[5] Unlike pre-modern societies which constituted

---

[3] Roberto Schwarz, *Ao vencedor as batatas: forma literária e processo social nos inícios do romance brasileiro* [Misplaced Ideas: Essays on Brazilian Culture], Duas Cidades/Editora 34, São Paulo, 2000, pp. 9–31.

[4] For an overview, see Silviano Santiago, *Intérpretes do Brasil* [Interpreters from Brazil], Nova Aguilar, Rio de Janeiro, 2002, vol. 1, pp. XIII–XLVIII.

[5] Marcelo Neves, *Transconstitucionalismo* [Transconstitutionalism], WMF Martins Fontes, São Paulo, 2009, pp. 26 ff.; Marcelo Neves, *Entre Têmis e Leviatã: uma relação difícil – o Estado democrático de direito a partir e além de Luhmann e Habermas* [Between Têmis and Leviathan: A Difficult Relationship – The Democratic State of Law to Depart and Beyond Luhmann and Habermas], WMF Martins Fontes, São Paulo, 2012, pp. 215 ff. See Niklas Luhmann, "Die Weltgesellschaft" [The World Society], in Niklas Luhmann, *Soziologische Aufklärung 2: Aufsätze zur Theorie der Gesellschaft* [Sociological Enlightenment 2: Essays on the Theory of Society], Westdeutscher Verlag, Opladen, 1975; Niklas Luhmann,

---

territorially-delimited formations, the globalisation of society developed from the sixteenth century on, intensified during the nineteenth century and was consolidated at the end of the twentieth century with the affirmation, including in the semantic sphere of self-description, of world society through the discourse of globalisation.[6] Even though the economic system originally propelled the emergence of world society, the latter is not merely a characteristic of capitalism or the economic system.[7] A main characteristic of world society is that the horizon of communications and expectations becomes, *primarily*, global, not limiting itself to a determined territory.

This is why the relationship between semantics and structure should be considered, primarily, from the point of view of the world society. Considering semantics as "a socially available sense that is generalized on a higher level and relatively independent from specific situations",[8] one may inquire how semantic constructions could assert themselves as self-descriptions of world society taking into account the presence, in this society, of such distinct situations on the structural plan (socially-stabilised expectations). A semantic artefact of global society may change in view of its adjustment to the reproduction of structures in diverse social contexts. Moreover, it is important to distinguish between semantics which refers to cognitive structures and semantics which refers to normative structures.

Since the cognitive structures of economics, technique and science do not segmentally differ in the sphere of world society, the predominant semantics in these domains have the potential of presenting themselves emphatically on a global level, with regional structural differences being of little importance. Therefore, the local, alternative semantics are widely neutralized, since they remain subordinated to the semantics of global society:

Die Gesellschaft der Gesellschaft [The Company of the Company], Suhrkamp, Frankfurt, 1997, pp. 145–171.

[6] Neves, 2009, see *supra* note 5, pp. 27–28. See Luhmann, 1997, *supra* note 5, p. 148; Hauke Brunkhorst, "Heterarchie und Demokratie" [Heterarchy and Democracy], in Hauke Brunkhorst and Peter Niesen (eds.), *Das Recht der Republik* [The Right of the Republic], Suhrkamp, Frankfurt, 1999, p. 374.

[7] See Luhmann, 1997, *supra* note 5, pp. 158–159; with objections to the concept of capitalism as a "world system" as proposed by Immanuel Wallerstein, *World-Systems Analysis: An Introduction*, Duke University Press, London, 2006.

[8] Niklas Luhmann, *Gesellschaftsstruktur und Semantik: Studien zur Wissenssoziologie der modernen Gesellschaft* [Social Structure and Semantics: Studies on the Sociology of Knowledge of Modern Society], Suhrkamp, Frankfurt, 1980, vol. 1, p. 19.

---

self-description of production, circulation, market, competitiveness, efficiency and so on. However, with regard to the normative structures of law and politics, territorial segmentation into states raises not only the question of the confrontation between world semantics and such varied structures, but also the problem of semantic artefacts which refer to normative structures that are reproduced in the respective state.

Within the world semantics of liberalism there is an aspect related to cognitive structures that serves the self-description of the capitalist economy, with a strong tendency to neutralise semantic alternatives. By its turn, constitutionalism as a legal-political semantics has a strong normative dimension. This means that, during the nineteenth and twentieth centuries, the liberal semantics of world society were not only submitted to tests of adequacy in light of normative structures of the states in which they were adopted, but were also pervaded by local semantics which subverted, to a large extent, their original meanings and functions. Certain shifts transmute ideas. Based on these suppositions, I shall present some general ideas on the semantics that refers to the constitutionalism experience at the turn of the nineteenth century to the twentieth century. Instead of 'misplaced ideas', would it not be important to inquire into the meaning and function of the development of *ideas in another place* or, better still, in various places of the global society? Would society *in* Brazil at the turn of the nineteenth century to the twentieth century – delimited by the state as a territorial legal-political organisation – not be one of these places in which constitutional ideas not only radiated themselves as pertaining to the dominant or hegemonic semantics of world society in relation to the normative structures, but were also confronted with local anti-liberal semantics? And what is the meaning of the trans-constitutional turn in Brazil?

6.2.   From Peripheral Constitutionalism

Here I shall offer a historical overview on the development of Brazilian constitutional law as an experience of peripheral constitutionalism within the world society.

While tolerating slavery, establishing a widely exclusionary census electoral system (under Articles 92 to 95) and adopting the 'Moderating Power' of the Emperor (Articles 98 to 101), an absolutist remnant, the Brazilian Imperial Constitution of 1824 expressed liberal traits, especially in the bill of rights contained in Article 179. But civil and political rights established in the constitutional document attained a very limited level of achievement and enforcement. The constitutional procedures have also undergone a profound "misrepresentation" in the implementation process. As an example, the widespread electoral fraud,[9] which was closely linked to pseudo-parliamentary practice developed during the Second Reign from 1840 to 1889, showed a reversal in the process of 'political will formation'.[10] In this context, the notion of constitutionality could not find space in the practice of the state agents and bodies themselves. Not only through ordinary legislative activity, which was incompatible with constitutional clauses, but also in the 'informal' practice of rulers, the Constitution was not conceived as the legal horizon of political and administrative actions.[11] That is why the constitutional review of laws, which, according to the Constitution, could have been exercised by the 'Moderating Power', was never developed; and when it has occurred, it was an "unconstitutional control of constitutionality" of local legislative acts by simple ministerial warnings (known as *avisos*).[12]

---

[9] See João Pandiá Calógeras, *Formação histórica do Brasil* [Historical Formation of Brazil], Editora Nacional, São Paulo, 1980, especially p. 270; Raymundo Faoro, *Os donos do poder: formação do patronato político brasileiro* [Owners of Power: Formation of the Brazilian Political Patronage], Globo, Porto Alegre, 1984/1985, pp. 364–387; Raymundo Faoro, *Machado de Assis: a pirâmide e o trapézio* [Machado de Assis: The Pyramid and the Trapeze], Editora Nacional/Secretaria de Cultura, Ciência e Tecnologia do Estado de São Paulo, São Paulo, 1976, pp. 127–163; João Camilo de Oliveira Tôrres, *A Democracia Coroada (Teoria Política do Império do Brasil)* [The Crowned Democracy (Political Theory of the Brazilian Empire)], José Olympio, Rio de Janeiro, 1957, pp. 283 ff.

[10] This state of affairs is usually expressed by a sort of logical sequence formulated by Senator Nabuco de Araújo, as cited in Joaquim Nabuco, *Um estadista do Império* [A Statesman of the Empire], Topbooks, Rio de Janeiro, 1936, vol. 1, p. 81; and Faoro, 1976, see *supra* note 9, p. 132: "The Moderating Power can call whom it wants to organize the council of ministries; this person makes the election because he has to do it; this election makes the majority." Cf. João Camilo de Oliveira Tôrres, *O Presidencialismo no Brasil* [The Presidentialism in Brazil], O Cruzeiro, Rio de Janeiro, 1962, p. 99.

[11] See Marcelo Neves, *Verfassung und Positivität des Rechts in der peripheren Moderne: Eine theoretische Betrachtung und eine Interpretation des Falls Brasilien* [Constitution and Positivity of Law in Peripheral Modernity: A Theoretical View and Interpretation of the Case of Brazil], Duncker und Humblot, Berlin, 1992, pp. 196–197.

[12] José Carlos Rodrigues, *Constituição Política do Império do Brasil* [Political Constitution of the Empire of Brazil], Laemmert, Rio de Janeiro, 1863, pp. 183–188.

The lack of legal implementation of the constitutional text did not imply a lack of actual politico-symbolic importance for the imperial power. In this sense, Gilberto Amado had already emphasised as follows: [13]

> It's clear that the "Constitution" being raised aloft, without having any contact with it [the people], could only be a fiction, a rhetoric symbol intended to be used by the speakers.

In the same line of interpretation, Faoro stressed that the Constitution was reduced "to a promise and a decorative panel".[14] That circumstance did not imply in any way the irrelevance of the 'Charter' as a "decorative panel", since the "fake world" of the 'Constitution' worked once again very efficiently in the "real world" of the factual power relations.[15] Not only in the constitutionalist rhetoric of governments, but also in oppositional speeches in defence of constitutional values offended by the governmental practice, the 'Imperial Charter' played an important political and symbolic function.[16] The legal inefficacy of the constitutional text was counterbalanced by its political effectiveness as a symbolic mechanism of 'legitimacy'.

The Constitution of 1891 did not reduce the problem of discrepancy between the Constitution and the reality of the power process. Rather, the most comprehensive statements of rights, freedoms and liberal principles embodied an even more intense contradiction between the constitutional document and the social structure than during the imperial experience.[17]

---

[13] Gilberto Amado, *As Instituições políticas e o meio social no Brazil* [Political Institutions and the Social Environment in Brazil], Imprensa Nacional, Rio de Janeiro, 1917, p. 30.

[14] Faoro, 1976, see *supra* note 9, p. 63; Aurelino Leal, *História Constitucional do Brasil* [Constitutional History of Brazil], Imprensa Nacional, Rio de Janeiro, 1915, pp. 146, 149.

[15] Faoro, 1976, see *supra* note 9, p. 175.

[16] In this sense, as Faoro asserts in his political and sociological interpretation of the literary work of Machado de Assis in Faoro, 1976, see *supra* note 9, pp. 65–66: "The Constitution would only be venerated by politicians in the opposition, who, in government – to be government – violated it, taking over the instruments of power that it only nominally limited. The exercise of government would always be the violated Constitution – hence the picturesque hollow cry of the opposition: 'plunge into the constitutional Jordan'".

[17] Although, see for another perspective (in the search for the identity of the 'Brazilian society'): Sérgio Buarque de Holanda, *Raízes do Brasil* [Roots of Brazil], José Olympio, Rio de Janeiro, 1988. Buarque de Holanda was aware of this issue and noted that, with the implementation of the Republic, the State "was uprooted" even more from the country. Further, according to Faoro, "arbitrariness" was fortified: see Faoro, 1976, *supra* note 9, p. 64. See also José Murilo de Carvalho, *A construção da ordem/Teatro de sombras* [The Order

The permanent misrepresentation or violation of the Constitution throughout the period in which it was formally in force (that is, from 1891 to 1930)[18] can be seen as the most important feature of the political and legal reality of the First Republic. There were significant expressions of the lack of legal implementation of the constitutional text, such as: electoral fraud as a rule in the political game controlled by local 'oligarchies';[19] degeneration of presidentialism into so-called 'neo-presidentialism',[20] primarily through excessive declarations of martial law;[21] deformation of federalism through the 'governor's politics',[22] and abusive proclamation of federal intervention in member states.[23]

Among conservative critics, who advocated an authoritarian, corporative and nationalist state, the lack of legal implementation of the constitutional text of 1891 was denounced as a contradiction between 'constitutional idealism' and 'national reality'.[24] However, in their criticism of the

---

Building/Shadow Theater], Editora UFRJ/Relume Dumará, Rio de Janeiro, 1996, especially p. 379.

[18] See Cláudio Pacheco, *Tratado das Constituições Brasileiras* [Treaty of the Brazilian Constitutions], Freitas Bastos, Rio de Janeiro, 1958, vol. 1, pp. 240 ff.

[19] In this respect, see Neves, 1992, *supra* note 11, pp. 170–171.

[20] On this concept, see Karl Loewenstein, *Verfassungslehre* [Constitution Teaching], Mohr, Tübingen, 1975, pp. 62–66.

[21] See Rui Barbosa, *Comentários à Constituição Federal Brasileira* [Comments to the Brazilian Federal Constitution], Livraria Academica/Saraiva, São Paulo, 1933, vol. 2, pp. 373 ff.; Rui Barbosa, *Comentários à Constituição Federal Brasileira* [Comments to the Brazilian Federal Constitution], Livraria Academica/Saraiva, São Paulo, 1933, vol. 3, pp. 323 ff.

[22] On the so-called 'governor's politics', see, for example, Raymundo Faoro, *Os donos do poder: formação do patronato político brasileiro* [Owners of Power: Formation of the Brazilian Political Patronage], Globo, Porto Alegre, 1985, vol. 2, pp. 563 ff.; Edgard Carone, *A Primeira República (1889-1930): texto e contexto* [The First Republic (1889-1930): Text and Context], DIFEL, São Paulo, 1969, pp. 103 ff.; Edgard Carone, *A República Velha (Evolução Política)* [The Old Republic (Political Evolution)], DIFEL, São Paulo, 1971, pp. 177 ff. Fernando Henrique Cardoso calls it an 'oligarchic pact', see: "Dos governos militares a Prudente-Campos Sales" [From Military Governments to Prudente-Campos Sales], in Fausto Boris (ed.), *História geral da civilização brasileira* [General History of Brazilian Civilization], DIFEL, São Paulo, vol. 3, 1985, pp. 47 ff.

[23] See Barbosa, 1933, *supra* note 21, p. 17.

[24] In this respect, see primarily Oliveira Vianna, *O Idealismo da Constituição* [The Idealism of the Constitution], Editora Nacional, São Paulo, 1939, pp. 77 ff.; Alberto Torres, *A organização nacional: Primeira parte, A Constituição* [The National Organization: Part One, The Constitution], Editora Nacional, São Paulo, 1978.

'utopian idealism' of the constituent legislator, the symbolic significance of the constitutional document was not accurately considered; on the contrary, the accent was on the ingenuity of its good intentions.[25] Under these terms, the Constitution would be an expression of misplaced ideas. The question whether the so-called 'utopian idealism' was only adopted in the constitutional document insofar as the realisation of the corresponding principles was postponed to a remote future and, thus, the status quo was not threatened, was not part of the discussion. Furthermore, one cannot forget that the 'nominalist Constitution' of 1891 functioned as an artefact of symbolic identification of the Brazilian legal-political experience with that of the United States ('US'), creating an image of a 'democratic' and 'constitutional' Brazilian state as its model. At the very least, the rhetorical invocation of liberal and democratic values that were consecrated in the constitutional document worked to discharge the "owners of power", transferring to the supposedly "backward society" the "responsibility" or "blame" for disrespecting the Constitution.

In response to new political tendencies, the affirmation of socio-democratic values in a society characterised by relations between under-citizens (under-integration) and over-citizens (over-integration)[26] is the new symbolic variable that comes with the constitutional model of 1934, which settled the foundation of the 'Brazilian welfare state'.[27] In the face of authoritarian trends that appeared during the period in which the new Constitution was formally in force, which resulted in the 1937 coup, an experience of symbolic constitutionalisation[28] was not widely developed.

In 1937 – again under the impact of new waves in Europe, this time of autocratic feature – President Getúlio Vargas, who had been President since 1930, under the pretext of a reaction against political and social movements from the left and the right, organised a *coup d'etat,* creating the so-

---

[25] See, for example, Vianna, 1939, *ibid.*, pp. 81, 91, 111.

[26] In this regard, see especially Marcelo Neves, "Between Under-Integration and Over-Integration: Not taking Citizenship Rights Seriously", in Jessé Souza and Valter Sinder (eds.), *Imagining Brazil*, Lexington Books, Lanham, 2005, pp. 61–90.

[27] While maintaining the "advent of the Brazilian welfare state" with the Constitution of 1934, Bonavides and de Andrade did not consider the problem of symbolic constitutionalisation, see: Paulo Bonavides and Paes de Andrade, *História Constitucional do Brasil* [Constitutional History of Brazil], Paz e Terra, Brasília, 1989, pp. 325–327.

[28] On symbolic constitutionalisation, see Marcelo Neves, *Symbolische Konstitutionalisierung* [Symbolic Constitutionalisation], Duncker und Humblot, Berlin, 1998.

called 'Estado Novo' (that is, 'New State'), a dictatorship based on his own personal power. The very Constitution enacted by Vargas himself in 1937, with highly centralist and authoritarian traits, remained suspended due to a transitory clause, Article 186, which established the State of Emergency. Karl Loewenstein, who conducted a study about Brazil at that time, referred to it as a "stillborn" Constitution.[29] The 'Estado Novo' lasted until 1945, when, in light of internal movements for re-democratisation and international pressures deriving from the victory of the allied forces, Vargas was overthrown.

Symbolic constitutionalisation according to the model of a welfare state was resumed with the Constitution of 1946. In this context, it is symptomatic of the co-existence, on the one hand, of the list of proclaimed social-democratic values, and, on the other hand, the majority in the constituent assembly and main support base of the constitutional system in 1946 (the Social Democratic Party) linked closely to rural oligarchies. Such a paradoxical link between solemnly-adopted democratic values and underlying interests can be better understood when one considers that the realisation of the constitutional model is transferred to an uncertain future and attributed to be achieved by those themselves in power.[30] Therefore, it does not follow this seeming contradiction is a threat to the status quo. In this scenario, it is talking about "freedom to enact democracy",[31] but not as an interpretation strictly based on the intentions of politicians:[32] the connection of actions and communication processes that promoted the symbolic constitutionalisation of 1946 was conditioned by structural variables that made possible the "freedom" of "enacting" social democracy without risking the enactors. The Constitution, comparable to Western European

---

[29] Loewenstein, 1975, see *supra* note 20, p. 142. See also Loewenstein, 1975, p. 49; and, similarly, Ivair Nogueira Itagiba, *O Pensamento Político Universal e a Constituição Brasileira* [Universal Political Thought and the Brazilian Constitution], Tupy, Rio de Janeiro, 1947, vol. 1, p. 282; Cláudio Pacheco, *Tratado das Constituições Brasileiras* [Treaty of the Brazilian Constitutions], Freitas Bastos, Rio de Janeiro, 1958, vol. 1, p. 267.

[30] João Almino, *Os Democratas autoritários: Liberdades individuais, de associação política e sindical na Constituinte de 1946* [The Authoritarian Democrats: Individual Freedoms, of Political and Syndical Association in the Constituent Assembly of 1946], Brasiliense, São Paulo, 1980, p. 305; João Almino, *Era uma vez uma constituinte* [There was Once a Constituent], Brasiliense, São Paulo, 1985, pp. 70–71.

[31] Almino, 1980, *ibid.*, pp. 66–94.

[32] With a contrary approach, see Almino, 1985, *ibid.*, p. 77.

models, only worked as a political symbol insofar as social trends related to its widespread implementation do not arise.

The nominalism of this Constitution was patent. The appearance of movements promoting basic reform, at the end of the 1950s and beginning of the 1960s, in the context of the Cold War, led to internal and international reactions. Under the pretext of the Communist menace, a military authoritarianism was imposed in 1964, as is now generally agreed with the support of the US.[33] By means of several institutional acts, but especially Institutional Act No. 5 of 1968, which violated the constitutional texts of 1967 and predominated over the Amendment Constitutional 1969 (that is, it was a statute of supreme rank in the legal order of the military regime), an authoritarian and super-centralised system was established, despite the fact that the constitutional texts continued to call Brazil a Federative Republic.[34]

The symbolic constitutionalisation of social-democratic orientation is restored and fortified with the Brazilian Federal Constitution of 1988, which is still formally in force. With the exhaustion of the long period of 'authoritarian constitutionalism' started in 1964, the symbolic identification with the values of democratic constitutionalism ceased to be politically relevant only for critics of the old regime, becoming significant also for supportive groups. A certain degree of "constitutional idealism" underlies the pre-constituent belief in the "recovery of the legitimacy".[35] The social context of the Constitution to be enacted already pointed to insurmountable limits to its widespread implementation. Nothing prevented, however, a constitutionalist rhetoric on the part of all political persuasions; on the contrary, it seems that the more the real relations of power moved away from the social-democratic constitutional model, the more radical was the constitutionalist discourse.

In recent years, especially since the end of the 1990s, the belief in the constitutionalisation of law has become strong among mainstream

---

[33] See p. 104 below.

[34] Criticizing the title 'Federal Republic', Bonavides referred to the form of State of the military regime as a *de facto* unitary State, see: Paulo Bonavides, "O caminho para um federalismo das regiões" [The Road to Regional Federalism], in *Revista de Informação Legislativa* [Magazine of Legislative Information], 1980, vol. 65, pp. 118–119.

[35] Raymundo Faoro, *Assembléia Constituinte: a legitimidade recuperada* [Constituent Assembly: The Legitimacy Recovered], Brasiliense, São Paulo, 1981.

Brazilian jurists.[36] The argument is that it would have overcome the predominantly symbolic character of the Constitution. However, in this particular matter, the argument is based mainly on 'judicialization' of politics. It should be noted that this phenomenon is inseparable from an overly-politicising judiciary, especially the Federal Supreme Court, referring basically to issues of political struggle and around topics related to included groups, even when it comes to issues of indisputable moral relevance. The Judicial Review has focused on the vast majority in the defense of corporate interests of public servants, not on fundamental rights issues.[37] Concerning the right to health, judicial interventions have served the interests of members of the upper economic strata, in order to determine the Union, Member States and the municipalities to pay for expensive treatments, at the expense of social programmes committed to universal access according to the constitution.[38] Thus, it is said to be a 'symbolic judicialization'.[39]

Although certain programmes against poverty have worked efficiently, reducing to some extent the exclusion, and the fight against corruption in politics and law has been fortified, there are still forms of under-citizenship and over-citizenship, as well as systematic practices of public officials against the constitutional dictates, in a sense that the implementation of the Constitution is very limited. In the experience of the Brazilian state, the political and legal practice is still markedly developed at the margins of the Constitution.

---

[36] See Cláudio Pereira de Souza Neto and Daniel Sarmento (eds.), *A constitucionalização do direito: fundamentos teóricos e aplicações específicas* [The Constitutionalisation of Law: Theoretical Foundations and Specific Applications], Lumen Juris, Rio de Janeiro, 2007.

[37] Alexandre Costa and Juliano Zaiden Benvindo, *A Quem Interessa o Controle Concentrado De Constitucionalidade? – O Descompasso entre Teoria e Prática na Defesa dos Direitos Fundamentais* [Who is Interested in Concentrated Control of Constitutionality? – The Mismatch between Theory and Practice in the Defense of Fundamental Rights], 2014.

[38] Virgílio Afonso da Silva, *Taking from the Poor to Give to the Rich: The Individualistic Enforcement of Social Rights*, 2007.

[39] See Wálber Araújo Carneiro, "A Cidadania Tutelada e a Tutela da Cidadania: O Deslocamento da Função Simbólica da Constituição para a Tutela Jurisdicional" [The Guardianship of Citizenship and the Guardianship of Citizenship: The Displacement of the Symbolic Function of the Constitution for Jurisdictional Protection], in Wilson Alves de Souza, Wálber Araújo Carneiro and Fábio Periandro de Almeida Hirsch (eds.), *Acesso à Justiça, Cidadania, Direitos Humanos e Desigualdade Socioeconômica: Uma Abordagem Multidisciplinar* [Access to Justice, Citizenship, Human Rights and Socioeconomic Inequality: A Multidisciplinary Approach], Editora Dois de Julho, Salvador, 2013.

This is not to be seen as an isolated experience. The experiences of peripheral constitutionalism are, in general, not separable from the corresponding experiences of central constitutionalism. This is not only an issue of the colonial period.[40] In 'neo-colonial' and 'post-colonial' terms, the advances of constitutionalism in regard to legal and political inclusion in the dominant centres during the twentieth century were associated with strategic geo-political fighting positions, which presuppose fully anti-constitutional positions on the part of the same political agents in foreign countries. When, in 1963, the statute was passed providing for affirmative action in the US, the democratic government of Lyndon Johnson was busy at the same time in preparing, in conjunction with the Brazilian military, a coup to overthrow a democratically elected civilian government, which proposed political and social reforms in the search for new pathways to inclusion.[41] Moreover, the US supported oppression in the maintenance of the dictatorship: for instance, more than 300 Brazilians went to the US Army School of the Americas, located then in Panama (moved in 1984 to Fort Benning, Georgia), to learn more efficient methods for torture and for other serious violations of human rights with their US counterparts, as announced in December 2014 in the final report of the Truth Commission established by the Brazilian government.[42]

6.3. To Trans-constitutionalism

Trans-constitutionalism means that two or more legal orders or organisations, whether of the same kind or of different kinds, engage simultaneously in the same constitutional case or problem.[43] In the following explanation, I shall present some experiences of the Brazilian legal order with transconstitutionalism.

Trans-constitutional entanglements between international and Brazilian state legal order are developing in the relations between the 'Inter-

---

[40] In this regard, see Louis Sala-Molins, *Le Code noir ou le calvaire de Canaan* [The Black Code or Calvary of Canaan], Presses Universitaires de France, Paris, 1987, pp. 206 ff.; Louis Sala-Molins, *Dark Side of the Light: Slavery and the French Enlightenment*, Minnesota University Press, Minneapolis, 2005.

[41] See Marcos Sá Corrêa, *1964 visto e comentado pela Casa Branca* [1964 Seen and Commented by the White House], L. & PM, Porto Alegre, 1977.

[42] Brasil, *Relatório* [Report], Comissão Nacional da Verdade [National Truth Commission], Brasília, 2014, vol. 1, pp. 330 ff.

[43] For a detailed analysis, see Neves, 2009, see *supra* note 5.

American Human Rights System', introduced by the American Convention on Human Rights ('ACHR'), and the constitutional orders of the signatories that have ratified it.[44] In this context, it is not simply a matter of imposing the decisions of the Inter-American Court of Human Rights ('IACHR'), created and structured by Chapter VIII (Articles 52 to 69) of the ACHR, on national courts with constitutional competence. The national courts are also reviewing their jurisprudence in light of the Court's decisions. In Brazil, two matters are relevant.

The first deals with the collision between Article 7.7 of the ACHR and Article 5.LXVII of the Brazilian Constitution. While the latter provision allows civil imprisonment for indebtedness in the case of an unfaithful trustee, the above-mentioned provision of the ACHR prohibits it. In judging three cases on 3 December 2008, a majority of the Brazilian Supreme Court ruled that treaties and conventions on human rights, when not approved in accordance with the procedure stipulated in Article 5, § 3, of the Brazilian Constitution (identical to the procedure for passing a constitutional amendment),[45] have supra-legal but infra-constitutional standing.[46]

These cases sparked a broad debate about the incorporation of human rights treaties by the Brazilian legal order. One tendency in analysis of the case has been to advocate a solution based on the idea of unlimited internal validity for the above-mentioned provision of the ACHR, given that this norm would lead to an extension of the rights established in the Brazilian

---

[44] This Convention was adopted on 22 November 1969, at San Jose, Costa Rica, and entered into force on 18 July 1978, in accordance with Article 74, no. 2. On the discussion in Brazil, see Antônio Augusto Cançado Trindade, "Prefácio: A Corte Interamericana de Direitos Humanos: um testemunho para a história" [Preface: The Inter-American Court of Human Rights: A Testimony to the History], in Márcio Luís de Oliveira (ed.), *O sistema interamericano de proteção dos direitos humanos – interface com o direito constitucional* [The Inter-American System for the Protection of Human Rights – Interface with Constitutional Law], Del Rey, Belo Horizonte, 2007, pp. XVII–XLIII.

[45] Article 5(3), of the Brazilian Constitution reads as follows: "The international treaties and conventions on human rights approved by each house of Congress in two rounds by three-fifths of all members shall be equivalent to constitutional amendments."

[46] Supremo Tribunal Federal [Brazilian Supreme Federal Court], *Recurso Extraordinário 466.343-1 São Paulo* [Extraordinary Remedy 466.343-1 São Paulo], RE 466.343/SP; Supremo Tribunal Federal [Brazilian Supreme Federal Court], *Recurso Extraordinário 349.703 Rio Grande do Sul* [Extraordinary Remedy 349.703 Rio Grande do Sul] RE 349.703/RS; Supremo Tribunal Federal [Brazilian Supreme Federal Court], *Habeas Corpus 87.585-8 Tocantins*, HC 87.585/TO.

Constitution and that the law contained in it would therefore be in harmony with Article 5, § 2 of the Constitution.[47] However, even the restrictive interpretation of the provision's internal validity does not exclude a positive solution that extends fundamental rights in practice: the argument in favour of the ratified Convention's supra-legal and infra-constitutional validity served as a basis for a decision that, because the Constitution only allows unfaithful trustees to be imprisoned for debt,[48] infra-constitutional law could therefore decide freely on permission or prohibition, and if so, the ACHR had primacy over the Brazilian Civil Code.[49] Only maintenance of the orientation that had predominated previously in the Brazilian legal tradition (that is, the principle that ratified international acts have the same level of validity as ordinary law) could lead to an insuperable conflict between the Supreme Court of Brazil and the IACHR, since the Brazilian Civil Code came into force after ratification of the treaty, and the maxim *lex posterior derogat priori* would therefore apply.[50] If it had maintained that position, the Supreme Court would have broken off the constitutional

---

[47]   Position defended by Justice Celso de Mello, leading the dissent, with support from Antônio Augusto Cançado Trindade, *Tratado de direito internacional dos direitos humanos* [Treaty of International Law on Human Rights], Fabris, Porto Alegre, 2003, vol. 1, p. 513; Flávia Piovesan, *Direitos humanos e o direito constitucional internacional* [Human Rights and International Constitutional Law], Saraiva, São Paulo, 2008, pp. 51–77; Valério de Oliveira Mazzuoli, *Direito internacional: tratados e direitos humanos fundamentais na ordem jurídica brasileira* [International Law: Treaties and Fundamental Human Rights in the Brazilian Juridical Order], América Jurídica, Rio de Janeiro, 2001, pp. 147–150; Valério de Oliveira Mazzuoli, *Curso de direito internacional público* [Public International Law Course], Revista dos Tribunais, São Paulo, 2007, pp. 682–702. De Mello goes further to argue that treaties and conventions on human rights are supra-constitutional, see Celso de Mello, "O parágrafo 2° do artigo 5° da Constituição Federal" [Paragraph 2 of Article 5 of the Federal Constitution], in Ricardo Lobo Torres (ed.), *Teoria dos direitos fundamentais* [Theory of Fundamental Rights], Renovar, Rio de Janeiro, 2001, pp. 25–26. Article 5(2) of the Brazilian Constitution reads as follows: "The rights and guarantees expressed in this Constitution do not exclude others deriving from the regime and from the principles adopted by it, or from the international treaties to which the Federative Republic of Brazil is a party".

[48]   Article 5.LXVII of the Brazilian Constitution reads as follows: "There shall be no civil imprisonment for indebtedness except in the case of a person responsible for voluntary and inexcusable default on an alimony obligation and in the case of an unfaithful trustee".

[49]   Position defended by Justice Gilmar Mendes, in an opinion leading the majority, see: Gilmar Mendes, Inocêncio Mártires Coelho and Paulo Gustavo Gonet Branco, *Curso de direito constitucional* [Course of Constitutional Law], Saraiva/IDP, São Paulo, 2007, pp. 665 ff.

[50]   Jurisprudence consolidated by the Brazilian Supreme Court in the *Judgment of 1 June 1977*, RE 80.004/SE, 29 December 1977.

---

dialogue with the IACHR on their respective understandings of human and fundamental rights. The discussion that did take place, however, appears to have foregrounded an effort to form a transversal rationality that can prove acceptable to both the legal orders involved.

The second matter deals with the conflict between the IACHR's decision in the case of *Gomes Lund (and others) v. Brazil*[51] and the Brazilian Federal Supreme Court's decision on the validity of the 1979 Amnesty Law (Federal Law No. 6683/1979).[52] Although the Executive Power has accomplished the decision of the IACHR, instituting the National Truth Commission, which concluded its work successful in terms of historical memory,[53] a fundamental conflict remains between the Brazilian judicial power and the IACHR with regard to the validity of the Amnesty Law for state agents who perpetrated crimes against the humanity under the dictatorship (that is, between 1964 and 1985). The IACHR understands that the Amnesty Law was not received under the Constitution of 1988 and cannot be applied for such crimes and agents, while the Brazilian Supreme Court decided on the full validity of the Amnesty Law. This conflict does not mean, however, that reciprocal learning in this matter is impossible. From part of Brazil, there are main agencies fighting against the decision of Supreme Court, both state attorneys and judges of lower instance, but above all through an appeal for 'Amendment of Judgment' (known as *embargos de declaração*) filed by the Brazilian Bar Association before the Supreme Court.

Another aspect of trans-constitutionalism regards 'cross-references' and 'conversation' among courts in various nation-states via reciprocal references to decisions of courts in other states.

In Brazil, there is also a longstanding tradition of reference to foreign constitutional provisions, jurisprudence, and doctrine. Although the influence of the US has long prevailed, especially by virtue of the strong influence of its constitutional model on the origins of Brazilian constitutionalism, European constitutional law and jurisprudence are increasingly

---

[51] Inter-American Court of Human Rights, *Case of Gomes Lund et al. v. Brazil*, Judgment of 24 November 2010 (Preliminary Objections, Merits, Reparations, and Costs), Series C No. 219 (http://www.legal-tools.org/doc/a66e9e/).

[52] Supremo Tribunal Federal [Brazilian Supreme Federal Court], *Judgment of 29 April 2010*, ADPF 153/DF, 8 June 2010.

[53] See Brasil, *Relatório* [Report], Comissão Nacional da Verdade [National Truth Commission], Brasília, 2014, vols. 1-3.

invoked. German constitutionalism, in particular, has exerted significant influence more recently. It is true that, historically speaking, references to foreign constitutional texts, doctrine, and jurisprudence have largely been an expression of '*bacharelismo*',[54] figuring in 'rhetorical' judges' opinions as proof of erudition, without relevant links to the merits of the case in question. Recent jurisprudence, however, displays a tendency to include references to foreign constitutional texts and precedents as both *obiter dicta* and part of the *ratio decidendi*.

In more recent Brazilian experience, trans-constitutionalism with other legal orders has developed conspicuously in the Federal Supreme Court. In important decisions relating to fundamental rights, foreign constitutional jurisprudence is cited not only in the opinions of individual justices, but also in case dockets as part of the *ratio decidendi*. In upholding an appellant's conviction on charges of racism for publishing a book with anti-Semitic content regarding Holocaust denial in the historic *Ellwanger* case, for example, references to foreign constitutional jurisprudence in the reasoning used by the Plenary of the Supreme Court played a fundamental role. In their written opinions, the justices conducted a detailed discussion of court precedents, constitutional provisions and legislation from foreign

---

[54] 'Bacharelismo' refers to a predominance of 'bachareis' (university-educated professionals, especially lawyers), in political and cultural life. It is also used to refer to a preference for rhetoric over research not only among lawyers, but also among doctors, engineers, economists and other members of the liberal professions, see: Vamireh Chacon, *Da Escola do Recife ao Código Civil (Artur Orlando e sua geração)* [From the School of Recife to the Civil Code (Artur Orlando and his generation)], Simões, Rio de Janeiro, 1969, p. 21. According to Birman and Lehmann, "*bacharelismo* is a rhetorical style associated with useless knowledge of little practical value", "a type of rhetoric, a style of writing, oracular and archaic, which was prevalent in politics and high culture", see: Patrícia Birman and David Lehmann, "Religion and the Media in a Battle for Ideological Hegemony: the Universal Church of the Kingdom of God and TV Globo in Brazil", in *Bulletin of Latin American Research*, 1999, vol. 18, no. 2, p. 163. For a critique of the generalised and simplistic use of the term with regard to Brazilian jurists, see Nelson Saldanha, "O chamado 'bacharelismo' brasileiro: ensaio de revisão" [The So-called Brazilian 'Bacharelismo': Revision Essay], in *Convivium* [Survive], 1978, vol. XVII/21, pp. 477–484. On the various conceptions of 'bacharelismo', see Alberto Venancio Filho, *Das arcadas ao bacharelismo (150 anos de ensino jurídico no Brasil)* [From Arcades to Baccalaureate (150 Years of Legal Education in Brazil)], Perspectiva, São Paulo, 1977, pp. 271 ff.

states, with relatively little reference to domestic and international law precedents.[55]

A great number of other examples could be given of Supreme Court judgments that cite foreign cases, although they do not always do so as part of the *ratio decidendi*, but as a contribution to the underlying reasoning.

Another area of trans-constitutionalism relates to the relationship between state legal orders and legal orders that are transnational in the strict sense, that is, normative orders constructed primarily not by or from states but by private or quasi-public actors or organisations. Several cases of trans-constitutionalism between states and transnational legal orders could also be analysed here on a worldwide scale, such as the entanglements concerning *lex mercatoria*, *lex sportiva*, and *lex digitalis*. For present purposes, however, it is pertinent to consider a recent example concerning the relationship between the Fédération Internationale de Football Association ('FIFA') and Brazil in the matter of the last World Cup.

In this issue, one of the most relevant aspects concerns Brazilian laws for the protection of the child, youth and the elderly – based on constitutional provisions such as Articles 6, 24.XV, 203.I-II, and 227–230 – according to which the price of tickets for public events must be reduced in half for children, young and aged people, a provision not followed by the FIFA World Cup Regulation. Despite the first reactions of Brazilian public bodies against the claim of FIFA for instituting exceptions to these laws, which was deemed unconstitutional and contrary to the sovereignty of Brazil, the bargaining between FIFA and Brazilian public bodies led to the enacting of three statutes on the World Cup (Federal Laws No. 12.350/2010, No. 12.462/2011 and No. 12.663/2012) and one decision from the Supreme Court favouring the main claims presented by FIFA. Although the approach of the Brazilian governmental agencies was very controversial, that episode shows that a higher capacity to learn the transnational entanglements can deliver better solutions for the domestic interests and values supported by the Constitution. If only Brazilian agencies were not so resistant at the beginning of conversations, they could have attained better results from the perspective of the Brazilian Constitution.

---

[55] Supremo Tribunal Federal [Brazilian Supreme Federal Court], *Habeas Corpus 82.424 Rio Grande do Sul, Judgment of 23 November 2003*, HC 82.424/RS, 19 March 2004.

Besides the cases of bilateral trans-constitutionalism, there are increasing situations in which a constitutional problem involves more than two legal orders. Two examples are worth mentioning in the trans-constitutional experience of Brazil.

The first example is the case of imports of re-treaded tires to Brazil. This dispute touches on Brazilian constitutional law, the legal orders of Uruguay and Paraguay, the laws of Mercosur, and the legal order of the World Trade Organization ('WTO'). On 17 December 2007, the WTO Dispute Settlement Body ('DSB'), in adopting the WTO Appellate Body Report of 3 December 2007, which modified the Panel Report of 12 July 2007, upheld an appeal by Brazil to ban imports of re-treaded tires from the European Union based on arguments relating to protection of the environment. However, this decision established that the Brazilian policy of continuing to import re-treaded tires from Paraguay and Uruguay entailed discrimination and should therefore be abolished, and the DSB did not accept the Brazilian claim that the number of re-treaded tires imported from Paraguay and Uruguay was insignificant.[56] Later, the European Communities requested binding arbitration. An arbitration award by a WTO-appointed arbitrator determined that a reasonable period for Brazil to implement the DSB's recommendations and rulings was 12 months from the adoption of the Panel Report and Appellate Body Report on 17 December 2007, that is, by 17 December 2008.[57] The problem posed by the DSB's decisions was that the Mercosur Permanent Review Court had previously ruled against a petition from Argentina requesting a ban on imports of re-treaded tires from Uruguay, reaffirming earlier decisions, based on the understanding that such a

---

[56] World Trade Organization Appellate Body Report, *Brazil – Measures Affecting Imports of Retreaded Tyres*, WT/DS332/AB/R and WT/DS332/R, 3 December 2007 (http://www.legal-tools.org/doc/90797b/).

[57] World Trade Organization Award of the Arbitrator, *Brazil – Measures Affecting Imports of Retreaded Tyres*, WT/DS332/16, 29 August 2008 (http://www.legal-tools.org/doc/3c3225/). For more on this case, see Alejandro Daniel Perotti, "Quién paga los costos del incumplimiento de las sentencias del Tribunal Permanente de Revisión Mercosur? Responsabilidad del Estado por violación del Derecho de la integración" [Who Pays the Costs of Non-Compliance with the Judgments of the Mercosur Permanent Review Court? State Responsibility for Violation of the Right to Integration], in El Derecho (ed.), *Suplemento de Derecho Administrativo* [Administrative Law Supplement], Universidad Católica Argentina, Buenos Aires, 2009, pp. 1–8.

ban would infringe Mercosur legal principles.[58] Although the Brazilian Supreme Court ruled partially in favour of the WTO motion, prohibiting imports of re-treaded tyres in general but allowing for some exceptions when such imports were based on Mercosur laws and guaranteeing *res judicata*,[59] the situation points to the pressing problems of combating provincial constitutionalism in the Brazilian case. At the same time, it evidences the great difficulty of achieving a satisfactory solution for all the orders involved.

The second example of pluri-dimensional entanglement issues around human rights is the case of Brazilian indigenous communities where the killing of new-born babies is considered legitimate.[60] In this context, it is relevant to note the International Labour Organization's Convention 169 concerning Indigenous and Tribal Peoples in Independent Countries,[61] which states in Article 8(2):

> These peoples shall have the right to retain their own customs and institutions, where these are not incompatible with fundamental rights defined by the national legal system and with internationally recognised human rights [...].

This provision further complicates the collision between native local orders and the order of state fundamental rights and international human rights. A literal reading of the provision, applied to absolute protection of the lives of new-borns, would tend to lead to ethnocide against the respective indigenous communities. In such cases, it is necessary but not sufficient to engage in a complexly adequate re-reading of both state fundamental rights norms and international human rights norms. A superficial universalism of human rights, based in a linear fashion on a certain Western ontological conception of such rights, is incompatible with a constitutional 'dialogue' with indigenous orders that do not correspond to this model. On

---

58 Tribunal Permanente de Revisión del Mercosur, *Award 1/2005 of 20 December 2005*; Tribunal Permanente de Revisión del Mercosur, *Award 1/2007 of 8 July 2007*; Tribunal Permanente de Revisión del Mercosur, *Award 1/2008 of 25 April 2008*.

59 Supremo Tribunal Federal, *Judgment of 24 June 2009*, ADPF 101/DF, 4 June 2012. This was a majority decision, with only Justice Marco Aurélio dissenting.

60 For a detailed explanation and analysis, see Neves, 2009, *supra* note 5, pp. 222 ff., 265–266.

61 On this Convention, see the brief exposition by Rüdiger Wolfrum, "The Protection of Indigenous Peoples in International Law", in *Zeitschrift für ausländisches öffentliches Recht und Völkerrecht*, 1999, vol. 59, pp. 369–382.

the contrary, a refusal to engage in a constructive 'dialogue'[62] with indigenous orders on this issue is itself a violation of human rights, since it would entail the 'ultra-criminalisation' of the entire community of perpetrators of the acts concerned, indiscriminately affecting their bodies and minds by means of destructive interference. In such cases, what is required in the name of positive trans-constitutionalism is the willingness of state and international orders to experience the surprise of reciprocal learning from the experience of the other, the indigenous community in its self-understanding.

All these experiences with trans-constitutionalism involving the Brazilian state legal order point to the need to transcend provincial treatment of constitutional problems by states, without leading to a belief in the *ultima ratio* of international public law, transnational law, supranational law or extra-state local normative orders: not only the first two but also the rest may make mistakes when faced with constitutional issues, including human rights problems. Trans-constitutionalism should move away from any illusion of a search for definitive 'inviolate levels': internationalism as *ultima ratio*, in a new absolute hierarchisation; supranationalism as a legal panacea; transnationalism as fragmentation to cast off the shackles of the state; or localism as the expression of a definitively inviolate ethicality.

6.4. Final Comments

I would like to make three brief final comments.

First, despite all historically-conditioned problems concerning the realisation of constitutionalism in Brazil (see section 6.2.), I maintain that instead of a 'misplaced idea', it is more appropriate to say that the constitutionalism undertook different functions in the various political-legal *loci* organised into states; however, it belongs to the semantics of the world society in which it circulates. Thus, a conclusion: the constitutionalism in Brazil has been, paradoxically, an *idea in another place* (the society *in* the scope of the Brazilian state) and *in the same place* (the world society).

---

[62] 'Dialogue' here might have an analogous meaning to that formulated by Feyerabend in Paul K. Feyerabend, *Three Dialogues on Knowledge*, Basil Blackwell, Oxford, 1991, pp. 164–165: "It can show the effect of arguments on outsiders or on experts from a different school", as well as "demonstrate the chimerical nature of what we believe to be the most solid parts of our lives".

Second, although trans-constitutionalism is still a scarce normative resource of the world society, especially in virtue of the asymmetry of power between centres and peripheries of this society, it offers a higher potential for effective constitutionalisation of several legal orders under different cultural contexts than models of cosmopolitan constitutionalism of Eurocentric or Western-centric base, which are not able to learn from the other. Thus, the other conclusion: the involvement of Brazil in trans-constitutional processes presents itself as a viable way to overcome the peripheral conditions of the Brazilian constitutionalism, so that it can reduce its (still excessive) charge of political symbolism and fortify its (still scanty) legal normative force.

Third, going beyond the Brazilian case, the trans-constitutional approach can be seen as a driver for managing and overcoming the current global crisis. For instance, legal and political means for successfully dealing with problems concerning migration, environment, global criminality, and human rights are not to be found in any isolated legal or political order, be it a state, or an international, transnational, supranational or local extra-state one. Hence, trans-constitutionalism is not only a counter-point to nationalism, but it also goes beyond cosmopolitan global constitutionalism models and fragmentation analyses, which are privileged on the so-called 'Global North'. The emphasis is on the learning entanglements of several *loci* for co-operation and competition in pursuit of solutions to constitutional problems, especially in our current crisis. Instead of dropping bombs on the territories of the others and building national walls against the others in the name of human rights and democracy, trans-constitutionalism entails the recognition that the various legal orders entangled in the search for a solution to a constitutional problem case that is concomitantly relevant to all must pursue transversal forms of articulation in order to develop such a solution, each observing the others in an effort to understand its own limits and possibilities for contributing to the solution. Identity is thereby reconstructed inasmuch as alterity is taken seriously, always observing and learning with the other.

7

Playing with Time:
Constitutions in an Unstable Age

Tom Ginsburg*

7.1. Constitutions, Stability and Change

The great Frank Zappa once said:

> You can't be a real country unless you have a beer and an air-
> line. It helps if you have some kind of a football team, or some
> nuclear weapons, but at the very least you need a beer.

To this list, one might add a constitution. New countries, as their very first act, typically adopt a foundational document that purports to reflect their national values and establish a structure for stable governance. Thus, the world's newest country, South Sudan, marked its independence on 9 July 2011 with a new constitution. And wannabe countries, from Abkhazia to Cascadia (a secessionist movement in the northwest United States ('US')) to Sealand (a purportedly independent country on an abandoned military platform), adopt constitutions as well. Constitutions are supposed to play a symbolic role in binding the nation together and expressing status on the international stage.

Constitutions, it is typically assumed, are designed to last forever. Constitutions constrain political actors, and thus can be conceived of as regulating the future on behalf of the past. Yet, if there is one feature that describes our era, it is instability. The pace of social and political change is rapid, and perhaps accelerating. Uncertainty, volatility, and contingency are the order of the day. This puts significant pressure on all institutions, including political constitutions. Dynamism, flexibility and resilience are the necessary responses to rapid change, but we know little about what features facilitate them. Constitutions have to be flexible; yet their very purpose is to provide stability to the political system. Calibrating the right level of

---

*   **Tom Ginsburg** is Professor of International Law and Political Science at University of Chicago.

stability, then, is critical. Managing the tension between stability and instability will be the central challenge for national constitutions in years ahead;
some might say it has been the central challenge for the last 230 years since
the American Constitution was adopted.

In this essay, we consider the search for an optimal level of flexibility,
and then discuss techniques which have proliferated to manage constitutional impermanence. We consider amendment, interpretation, and replacement as three options, identifying trends and trade-offs. We then turn to the
design of iterated constitutional negotiations as a different model that is
emerging.

7.2. Optimal Flexibility?

What is the right level of constitutional flexibility? Two centuries ago, some
three decades after the founding of the US, Thomas Jefferson bemoaned
those who fetishize constitutions. As he wrote:

> Some men look at constitutions with sanctimonious rever-
> ence, and deem them like the arc of the covenant, too sacred
> to be touched. They ascribe to the men of the preceding age a
> wisdom more than human, and suppose what they did to be
> beyond amendment. I am certainly not an advocate for fre-
> quent and untried changes in laws and constitutions. I think
> moderate imperfections had better be borne with; because,
> when once known, we accommodate ourselves to them, and
> find practical means of correcting their ill effects. But I know
> also, that laws and institutions must go hand in hand with the
> progress of the human mind. As that becomes more devel-
> oped, more enlightened, as new discoveries are made, new
> truths disclosed, and manners and opinions change with the
> change of circumstances, institutions must advance also, and
> keep pace with the times. We might as well require a man to
> wear still the coat which fitted him when a boy, as civilized
> society to remain ever under the regimen of their barbarous
> ancestors.

Jefferson's view has inspired radical democrats, though it has not
been popular in his home country, where the Constitution is venerated with
a respect near to that of the Bible. A major school of constitutional interpretation – originalism – retains popularity precisely because of veneration
of the ancients. Its adherents scour historical evidence for indicators that
one or the other founder meant something close to the interpreters preferred

meaning. Jefferson would surely have been an advocate of the alternative theory of 'living constitutionalism'. The latter, which has been embraced by many constitutional courts and the European Court of Human Rights, is a mechanism of evolution.

The fact is that in most other countries, constitutions are not so venerated and constitutional change is a fact of life. This may be because of frequent amendments; some countries like Mexico, Brazil, India, and Pakistan amend their constitutions virtually every year. In others, constitutions are replaced. My co-authors and I have shown that tearing up a constitution and starting over is a remarkably frequent occurrence in much of the world. We estimate that on average, constitutions can be expected to last an average of 19 years, hardly enough to provide a stable basis for politics.[1]

Consider several mechanisms of constitutional change and adjustment: amendment, interpretation, and replacement. Amendment rules are of course internally provided for in the constitutional scheme. Amendment mechanisms vary wildly across countries, as do rates. However, we observe an increase in the frequency of amendment since 1950, suggesting that there is indeed increasing resort to formal constitutional adjustment in the face of more rapid change.[2]

It is sometimes argued that the US Constitution is the world's most difficult to amend. But in fact the basis for that claim is unclear. It is tricky to compare across countries. The US constitutional formula involves, most commonly, two-thirds of both houses of Congress, and three-fourths of the state legislatures. But is this really more difficult than the Japanese formula of two-thirds of the legislature and a public referendum? It is hard to tell. The US Constitution has been amended more frequently than the Japanese Constitution, which has never been changed. Indeed, cross-national research suggests there is little correlation between institutional structure and actual amendment rate, though methodological difficulties abound.[3]

---

[1]   Zachary Elkins, Tom Ginsburg, and James Melton, *The Endurance of National Constitutions*, Cambridge University Press, New York, 2009.

[2]   Tom Ginsburg and James Melton, "Does the constitutional amendment rule matter at all?: Amendment Cultures and the Challenge of Measuring Amendment Difficulty", in *International Journal of Constitutional Law*, 2015, vol. 13, no. 3, pp. 686–713.

[3]   *Ibid.*

Still, if change is accelerating because of social and technological disruptions, this argues for a relatively flexible amendment formula. My own view is that, while a super-majority requirement is a good one, it should not be so high as to block constitutional change. To be sure, the recent experience in Hungary provides a counter-argument. In Hungary, a brief victory by the Fidesz party after the financial crisis allowed the party to change the Constitution towards entrenching its rule forever. This was a harbinger of a rightward, illiberal turn in Eastern European politics, which increasingly resemble the Putin model of electoral authoritarianism. These countries have attacked courts and sought to implement limitations on the rule of law.[4] One could argue that a higher threshold for amendment would have saved the day. But, ultimately, this is a problem of competing risks: the risk of a temporary majority locking in its power must be balanced against the risk that excessive rigidity leads actors to tear up the constitution in its entirety. And some countries in Eastern Europe have pivoted east even without constitutional reform.

Another mechanism of adjustment is constitutional interpretation by courts. With the spread of constitutional review around the globe, this is becoming quite a common mechanism of constitutional change. Yet, it too has problems, most obviously normative ones. Who, after all, elected the judges to be the ones to make fundamental law? (We set aside the interesting case of Bolivia, where constitutional court judges really are elected.) Interpretative change is critical, even essential to adjusting to rapidly-changing conditions. Yet its legitimacy is often questioned. Still, it is apparent that constitutional and supreme courts around the world are exercising powers that would have been unthinkable just a few decades ago. This has facilitated, in some countries, constitutional responsiveness to various trends, as well as limitations on governments of all stripes. It is surely one of the most significant developments in governance in the last few decades.

A third approach to adjustment is constitutional replacement. As mentioned above, this is remarkably frequent and most constitutions die at a relatively young age. However, it leaves a good deal to be desired as a normative model. After all, it requires starting from scratch. Constitutions are, at bottom, essentially political bargains between forces that usually

---

4   Bojan Bugaric and Tom Ginsburg, "The Assault on Postcommunist Courts", in *Journal of Democracy*, 2016, vol. 27, no. 3, pp. 69–82.

have fundamental disagreements. Parties come together to bargain, and may, if circumstances and relationships are aligned, conclude a deal. The document serves as a focal point, allowing parties to co-ordinate their expectations of the other side, and establishing institutions for ongoing governance. If a constitution functions well, the parties may gradually develop trust, and may submit to the jointly established institutions for effective ongoing governance. If it does not function well, and if mistrust remains high, the agreement may break down. Reaching agreement in the first place is hard, as shown by the hundreds of failed constitutional bargains that never see the light of day. The point is that replacement is not generally recommended: if we assume that negotiation is costly, then getting rid of a constitution even for major flaws might be throwing out the baby with the bathwater.

7.3.   Iteration as a Solution

When faced with a major and complex bargaining problem, one approach that is sometimes used in the world of business is to break the problem down into smaller parts. By analogy, we are increasingly seeing constitutional negotiations extended across multiple iterations. Instead of a single big bang negotiation with everything on the table, constitutional negotiation can take the form of several rounds of bargaining, with each step leading to a next one.

What might this look like? One place to look is the Constitution of the European Union itself, which emerged from several different rounds of treaty negotiations, moving, until recently, toward "an ever closer Union". While that particular example is losing its lustre, the model has also been used in various transitional situations, such as Iraq, Somalia and South Sudan. Israel has proceeded this way since its founding, as has Canada, which lacks a single consolidated 'constitution'. Both countries have adopted a series of major statutes that serve higher goals than 'ordinary' law.

Transitional, interim or temporary constitutions are clear examples. In this model, the constitutional document is explicitly limited in time, designed to last only for a short time, not forever. The key element is that the framework provides for drafting a final constitution. Such arrangements are desirable when more permanent agreement is either impossible for political reasons, or unwise for other reasons. What might such reasons be? A basic problem is that of information. At the moment in which any regulation is passed, we do know for certain what the future holds. Conditions may change, and we may not be confident about which challenges we will have to address in the future. The greater the volatility or variance in expected outcomes, the more there is a case to be made for deciding only a limited number of issues. This point has obvious implications for our moment of rapid change.

Furthermore, in a situation of political bargaining, we might not know the intentions of the other side. In South Sudan, for example, an interim constitution was negotiated with the rump state of Sudan, but also divisions between forces loyal to President Salva Kiir and those loyal to Vice President Riek Machar. While Machar and Kiir were able to co-operate when the antagonist was Omar al Bashir, once their secessionist project succeeded, new cleavages became apparent and the internal divisions manifested themselves, leading to an appalling war. When they were negotiating with each other, neither Machar nor Kiir could be sure the other would defect from the co-operative equilibrium. This meant that their trust in each other was limited. This kind of bargaining problem might also lead them to want to leave some issues off the table for subsequent negotiations.

Perhaps in such circumstances, narrower, more limited arrangements are advisable. By temporally limiting the arrangements, one lowers the stakes. Interim constitutional arrangements involve the manipulation of temporality, limiting duration of what is supposed to be an enduring form. They are proverbial bridges, over which the polity must pass to get to temporally permanent institutions.

Like narrow bridges, interim arrangements are somewhat fragile. If they work well, they can establish patterns of trust among political antagonists. If they break down, however, they can stall the transition to a new regime. Like narrow bridges, they must not be over-burdened. Ideally, they should provide for both incentives and procedures to adopt a final constitution, and not be too constraining.

This point about calibrating the level of content and constraint in a constitutional text is more general. In some circumstances, it will be wise to decide *not* to decide every issue in a constitution. Drafting techniques can, for example, call for certain issues to be resolved in ordinary law rather than in the constitutional text.[5] In some other cases, they might provide for particular deadlines to be met, without deciding the substance of the decision. This allows for new information to be revealed over time, helping to ensure that the constitution is responsive. It is another form of ensuring that the text is not too rigid.

Another technique is to have a mandatory review of the constitution some years after passage. In one prominent example, Brazil's constitution-makers promised a referendum on the issue of whether the country should retain presidentialism or adopt parliamentarism five years after adoption of the Constitution. In the event, the voters decided to retain presidentialism, but the technique of mandatory review provided for a nice, clean way to make a change if the experience had been revealed to be problematic. (Today, Brazil's voters might be wishing they had gone the other way.)

All these drafting techniques involving manipulation of time have been especially useful in transitional situations where political agreement is very challenging. In Iraq, for example, a Transitional Administrative Law gave way to a 'permanent' Constitution, produced under severe American pressure, which in turn left many issues off the table because the country's political forces were not ready to reach agreement. The country's federal structure, the division of oil, and the composition of the upper house of the legislature were all issues that the constitutional text did not resolve. Instead, these were to be dealt with through mandatory constitutional revision and the passage of organic statutes. In many cases, these never materialized. This suggests that leaving issues off the table is not a panacea or a substitute for political agreement.

7.4. Implications for Global Governance

We are in an era of rapid change in society, politics and economy. It is not surprising, then, that constitutions have also come under pressure to adjust with the times. There are certain mechanisms internal to constitutions that provide the documents with the necessary resilience to survive in a world of rapid change. These include relatively loose amendment rules, or flexible approaches to constitutional interpretation. But there are also new developments in the ways that constitutions are produced that seem appropriate for

---

[5] Rosalind Dixon and Tom Ginsburg, "Deciding Not to Decide: Deferral in Constitutional Design", in *International Journal of Constitutional Law*, 2012, vol. 9, pp. 636–672.

an era of contingency and change. Instead of being a single big-bang nego-tiation, we observe constitutional bargaining extended over long periods of time. This has great advantages from a functional point of view, but also may undermine constitutions' ability to embody the nation and to bring di-verse people together. Still, recognising that constitutions unfold over time is a valuable point in a world of constant change. Instead of a complete product, constitutions can be thought of as a process.

In this sense, developments in the field of national constitutions have implications for broader problems in global governance. The global gov-ernance project has in many ways come to resemble a dysfunctional or out-moded constitutional bargain. In many countries, a major populist backlash has arisen against transnational trade and investment; multilateral ap-proaches have not been particularly good at dealing with basic problems of peace and security; the spectre of climate change has not been squarely confronted; and the legitimacy of the global order seems to be in crisis. Regional organisations are losing members, not gaining them; and one speaks of crisis at institutions like the International Criminal Court.

A constitutional perspective offers a set of options for some of these problems. In any given area, one could start over, trying to create a global 'new deal' with new institutions, perhaps after a systematic review of the old ones; one might adopt a more flexible set of arrangements that can ad-just to changing conditions; or one could instead break down problems of international co-operation into discrete component parts, hoping that pat-terns of co-operation might emerge when relatively low stakes issues are tackled. Each of these has been used at various times in the international community. None is a panacea for our moment, but in some areas, these approaches might be quite worthwhile.

Consider global co-operation. The rigidity of treaty regimes has led some to say that the treaty is dead as a tool for multilateral governance.[6] But what if treaty regimes were designed with mandatory reviews, and mechanisms for adjusting the bargain over time? States might be less re-luctant to enter into them, and the treaty regimes could consist of forums for iterated bargaining rather than hard constraints. Sunset provisions, too,

---

[6] See Duncan Hollis, "The End of Treaties? The End of History?", in *Opinio Juris*, 29 April 2014.

would be a design technique capable of being deployed more frequently in international affairs.[7]

Ultimately, though, constitutions and international arrangements share the quality of being formal and somewhat technical documents. To succeed and endure, they require political support and sustenance. It is this that is the major challenge of our era, for both national and international institutions.

[7] Barbara Koremenos, *The Continent of International Law: Explaining Agreement Design*, Cambridge University Press, Cambridge, 2016.

8

Reflections on Global Strategies to Combat Transnational and International Crime

Philip L. Reichel*

Understanding the incidence of crime and the search for efforts to prevent or combat its occurrence has intrigued and befuddled scientists, politicians, policy-makers, and practitioners since the earliest concerns for collective security. Only recently have those concerns moved beyond domestic crime. The term 'transnational crime' was first used by criminologists during the 1970s, when the concept of transnationalism was entering the vocabulary of many social sciences. An early use – if not the first – occurred during the Fifth United Nations Congress on Crime Prevention in 1975, when the term was used to guide discussion at the conference.

Over the next several decades, the idea being conveyed by the term 'transnational' was more widely accepted than was the word's meaning. Reference to international crime or global crime often seemed indistinguishable from discussion of transnational crime. Further complications arose when the concept of organised crime was included in the conversation.

Beyond the issues related to 'what', there are also questions about 'who' and 'how' in a discussion of security at the global level. That is, who is responsible for assuring our security and how do they go about that task? At the global level it would be helpful (even if not desirable) to be able to answer 'the global police' and 'by constantly monitoring all the world's population'. Less flippantly, concerns with *what, who,* and *how,* when discussing the very broad issue of world-wide strategies regarding transnational/international/global crime requires initial attention to some definitions. To that end, this contribution begins by operationalising a few key

---

*   **Philip L. Reichel** is Professor Emeritus of Sociology and Criminal Justice at the University of Northern Colorado, Adjunct Professor at the University of New Hampshire Law School, and Visiting Professor at the University for Peace (a United Nations-mandated university).

terms so readers will have an understanding of how the topic is being approached. That task is followed by a section on the current global legal environment regarding international and transnational crime and a section on some likely developments regarding efforts at combating those crimes.

8.1. Defining Terms

Domestic crime is easily understood as referring to crime within a particular country. That concept was quite sufficient until criminologists and others began paying attention to criminal activities that clearly involved more than one country. When a victim is kidnapped in Country A, transported through Country B, and killed in Country C, the concept of domestic crime seems inadequate. Or, what about industrial pollution that is taken by wind across country borders and results in clear harm to citizens of another country. Equally problematic are cyber criminals who sit at a computer in one country as they commit a fraudulent act against a person at a computer in another country.

Most criminologists and others would agree that each of those examples is a crime that goes beyond what is typically considered to be 'domestic' (although the pollution example as crime would be controversial). Some have referred to such acts as 'global crime' whereas others have preferred the terms 'international crime' or 'transnational crime'. Today, and here, the described acts are called transnational crime. 'Global crime' is more often used by criminologists to explain crime's distribution rather than its typology. 'International crime' is increasingly used in reference to acts that threaten the world order and security – with the primary examples being crimes against humanity, war crimes, genocide, and for some, terrorism – and may or may not involve multiple countries. 'Transnational crime' is more typically used for crimes that affect the interests of more than one state and are committed for personal gain and profit. Albanese succinctly places various transnational crimes into one of three categories: Provision of illicit goods (for example, drug trafficking and counterfeiting), Provision of illicit services (such as human trafficking and cybercrime), and Infiltration of business or government (for instance, money laundering and corruption).[1]

---

[1] Jay S. Albanese, *Transnational Crime and the 21st century: Criminal Enterprise, Corruption, and Opportunity*, Oxford University Press, New York, 2011.

As indicated in the title of this contribution, attention here is on 'transnational crime' and 'international crime', as defined above. The title also announces global strategies to combat those crimes. Key here are the words "global strategies" and "combat". The comments below regarding "global strategies" are provided in the context of global governance as understood to be the different ways that governments, organisations, institutions, and businesses manage global affairs. Reference to the role of global governance in 'combating' transnational and international crime must emphasise collaboration over unification. That is, efforts to combat transnational crime requires governments, organisations, institutions, and businesses to work together across national boundaries, but does not require them to operate as a single entity (for example, by sharing resources but not creating a global police-force).

Given those definitional constraints, what can be said about the current global efforts to combat transnational and international crime, and what are some likely developments regarding efforts at combating those crimes?

8.2. Current Global Efforts Regarding International and Transnational Crime

Global efforts regarding international crime are most clearly linked to the International Criminal Tribunal for the Former Yugoslavia, the International Criminal Tribunal for Rwanda, and the International Criminal Court ('ICC'). Since its creation in 2002 and through April 2018, the ICC has undertaken 11 investigations, issued 32 arrest warrants, and has four successful convictions.[2] Almost all formal actions and convictions have been against black Africans – leading to a charge of bias by some observers (particularly the African Union). Further, the slow pace at which the ICC operates and the significant expense of its operation have also brought criticism to the Court. All told, an assessment of current global efforts regarding international crime suggests there is considerable room for improvement.

Views of current global efforts regarding transnational crime are more positive. There are, of course, a variety of international instruments that include bilateral and multilateral agreements such as the United Nations Convention on Transnational Organized Crime and the United

---

2   International Criminal Court, *The Court Today*, 23 April 2018.

Nations Convention against Corruption. Some agreements are more crime-specific (for example, the United Nations Convention against Illicit Traffic in Narcotic Drugs and Psychotropic Substances and the International Convention for the Suppression of the Financing of Terrorism). Agreements such as these have certainly been helpful in drawing attention to the crimes themselves, in assisting nations in developing laws regarding those crimes, and in developing protocols for action.

Whereas bilateral and multilateral agreements are necessary and important components for international co-operation, there are other ingredients that highlight more practical aspects. The primary mechanisms include co-operative law enforcement, mutual legal assistance, extradition, transfer of prisoners, and transfer of proceedings in criminal matters.[3] Co-operative efforts such as these are widespread at international and regional levels. Toolkits – especially those created by the United Nations Office on Drugs and Crime ('UNODC') – have been distributed to aid practitioners in sharing of best practices. Data is shared among law enforcement agencies (for instance, via Interpol and Europol). Various organisations (for example, the International Law Enforcement Academy and the European Police College) provide law enforcement training to multiple countries. Model laws (such as the UNODC's Model Law against Trafficking in Persons) assist governments in translating their obligations under international treaties into national legislative provisions. And, there is continued expansion of mutual legal assistance efforts (as seen from the European Convention on the Transfer of Proceedings in Criminal Matters, for example).

Those examples, and many more, provide clear indication that the world's nations do not lack for strategies that encourage and support cross-national co-operation. Problems do remain, however, and they are not insignificant. Issues of sovereignty are often raised, the ability (financial, technical, political and so on) of some countries to abide by agreements is difficult, human rights and privacy issues can be challenging to reconcile, and competition among agencies/organisations presents barriers. Consider

---

[3] Matti Joutsen, "International instruments on cooperation in responding to transnational crime", in Philip Reichel and Jay Albanese (eds.), *Handbook of Transnational Crime and Justice*, SAGE, Los Angeles, 2014, pp. 303–322; United Nations Office on Drugs and Crime and United Nations Human Settlements Programme, *Crime Prevention Assessment Tool: Criminal Justice Assessment Toolkit*, United Nations, New York, 2006 (http://www.legal-tools.org/doc/22b341/).

the cross-national efforts to combat human trafficking as illustrative of problems associated with other transnational crimes.

At the most basic level, cross-national co-operation to combat transnational crime requires the support of high level political officials, but also depends on the pre-existing intra-country co-operation. Unfortunately, in many countries where human trafficking occurs, there is insufficient intra-country co-operation among the various players to enable those countries to effectively participate in cross-national collaboration. Even when political will and sufficient intra-country co-operation is present, effective cross-national co-operation is not easily achieved. In a study of European agencies involved in cross-national efforts, I identified several impediments to cross-national co-operation that could be grouped under five categories:

1. *Problems related to corruption* explain that co-operative efforts are hindered when governments, organisations, or individuals are more interested in personal gain than in achieving the broader goal of co-operation endeavours toward combating the problem;

2. *Problems related to competition* remind us that competition among organisations for funding and recognition can hamper co-operative efforts since successful efforts by individual organisations can result in increased attention and additional funding;

3. *Problems related to differing legal systems* note that lack of knowledge about roles and procedures in another country's legal system can lead to confusion as to appropriate people to contact and procedures to follow;

4. *Problems related to evaluation* point to the absence proper programme evaluation and the resulting difficulty of knowing whether organisational efforts have been effective; and

5. *Problems related to approach*, call attention to the fact that collaboration can be hindered when some workers and organisations respond to human trafficking as primarily a human rights issue whereas others approach it from a crime control model.[4]

Although not inherently conflicting, the goals of each approach can clash.

---

[4] Philip Reichel, *Cross-National Collaboration to Combat Human Trafficking: Learning from the Experience of Others*, United States Department of Justice, 2008.

Those impediments to cross-national collaboration remind us that significant challenges remain as nations work together in response to transnational crime. The variety of international instruments and mechanisms are impressive in their number, variety, and adoption. Again, for illustration, consider the United Nations Protocol to Prevent, Suppress and Punish Trafficking in Persons, Especially Women and Children. The Protocol is imperfect and has certainly been criticised on a variety of points, but it also shows how current global efforts can be commended. Gallagher argues that the Protocol has done more than any other single legal development to place the issue of human exploitation firmly on the international political agenda and to provide a valuable road map for change.[5] It triggered unprecedented levels of action in international and regional agreements, and encouraged governments and civil society groups to became involved in researching the issue and initiating or supporting anti-trafficking efforts. Similar arguments can be made for other agreements and for the efforts of agencies/organisations involved in cross-national collaboration at combating transnational crime and responding to victims of those crimes.

In sum, it can be argued that current global efforts regarding international and transnational crime are robust yet continue to face serious impediments. Successes are apparent, but considerable work is required even to maintain current accomplishments.

8.3. Likely Developments Regarding Co-operative Efforts and Their Focus

As noted earlier, the ICC is the primary organisation charged with responding to international crime. Whereas the ICC can certainly point to some successes, it seems likely that critics will increasingly voice their concerns. For example, McCargo notes that a cumbersome international judicial process simply may not be the best approach.[6] He argues that the international community should get out of the business of putting people on trial and suggests that independent national inquiries with prosecution by the national courts may be the more viable and realistic route. It seems quite likely that concerns and solutions of this type will continue to be raised in the

---

[5] Anne T. Gallagher, "Two Cheers for the Trafficking Protocol", in *Anti-Trafficking Review*, 2015, no. 4, pp. 14–32.

[6] Duncan McCargo, "Transitional Justice and its Discontents", in *Journal of Democracy*, 2015, vol. 26, no. 2, pp. 5–20.

coming years. However, it seems more likely to me that, rather than moving away from the ICC, it will undergo some reforms – especially in terms of having clearer and more realistic goals.

Developments and strategies regarding co-operative efforts toward transnational crime are more satisfying to consider. I would like to briefly emphasise three themes that I see as likely to attract attention in the coming years: emerging crimes, women in transnational crime, and the role of civil society and private business.

8.3.1. Emerging Crimes

Many of the transnational crimes currently identified as such are conventional criminal activities carried out across border. Among those, there are several that are likely to receive increased attention in the coming years. Authorities have been aware of – and concerned about – cybercrime and identity-related crime for years, but both categories of criminal activity are receiving increased media attention and that in itself will help keep them as law enforcement objectives. Similarly, human trafficking has been on the world agenda for decades, but often the emphasis was on trafficking for sex exploitation. Thanks to the efforts of groups such as the International Labour Organization,[7] there is increased attention on trafficking for labour exploitation and sophisticated research to support the findings.

Although it is sometimes included in the discussion of human trafficking generally, trafficking in human organs is increasingly studied and discussed as a separate activity. Traffickers exploit the desperation of both donors (usually trying to improve their economic situation) and recipients (who typically have few other options to improve or prolong their lives). As long as the demand for healthy organs exceeds supply, criminal enterprises will take advantage of the situation.

Whereas activities such as cybercrime and human trafficking are familiar examples of transnational crime, there are other activities that are more accurately included as examples of emerging transnational crimes – either because the activity itself is increasingly global or because the activity is more often recognised as being criminal. Examples include trafficking in fraudulent medicine, wildlife and forest crime, and the transnational movement of gangs.

---

[7] See the web site of the International Labour Organization.

Trafficking in fraudulent medicine poses a considerable public health threat since the result can be a failure to cure, may cause harm, and could even kill patients. Because the supply chain for medicines operates at a global level, cross-national co-operation is required to effectively detect and combat the introduction of fraudulent medicines along this supply chain. At present, criminal groups are taking advantage of the difficulties in international co-operation as well as the lack of resources of regulatory, enforcement and criminal justice officials, to make this newer form of transnational crime especially worrisome.[8]

Wildlife and forest crime is, most broadly, the illegal exploitation of the world's wild flora and fauna. The UNODC explains that this activity has transformed into one of the largest transnational organised criminal activities alongside drug trafficking, arms, and trafficking in human beings.[9] Because wildlife and forest crime severely impacts national security and social and economic development (as well as threatening biodiversity and endangered species), there is every reason to believe the activity will become more prevalent and greater attention will be directed to it.

Transnational gangs are not a new phenomenon, but they are typically linked to groups of people representing a particular race, ethnicity, or nationality. Today – and with a view to the future – the concern is with street, prison, and motorcycle gangs that increasingly have cross-border influence. Specific examples are the Mara Salvatrucha (MS-13) and the 18th Street gang (M-18). Both are considered transnational because their membership has spread from Los Angeles to communities across the United States ('US') and into Central America and Mexico. In all locations, they are engaged in criminal enterprises that pose security and public safety threats in individual neighbourhoods, metropolitan areas, nations, and across borders. US-based prison gangs – the Mexican Mafia being a prime example – are active in Canada, Mexico, and Central America. Their criminal activities are mostly drug-related and operate in prisons and other correctional facilities, but their influence can also extend into the community. Outlaw Motorcycle Gangs have been described as the only organised crime group developed in the US to be exported around the world. For example,

---

[8] United Nations Office on Drugs and Crime, *Trafficking in Fraudulent Medicine*, 2013, available on the web site of the UNODC.

[9] United Nations Office on Drugs and Crime, *Wildlife and Forest Crime: Overview*, available on the web site of the UNODC.

the Hells Angels, Bandidos and Outlaws now have more chapters outside than inside the US. The American-based biker gangs became more criminal as they and their drug links expanded beyond the US borders and, today, they present serious and ongoing crime threats in all their locations.[10]

Also of growing importance and concern is the overlap between transnational crime and terrorism. Reference to the transnational crime-terrorism nexus is increasing found in the literature as scholars, practitioners, and policy-makers come to understand how terrorist groups use such criminal activities as money laundering and drug trafficking to provide financial support for their activities.

There are, of course – and unfortunately – other crimes that are increasingly transnational in nature. The weaponization of infectious diseases, environment crime, and illegal sports betting and match fixing, come to mind. Those are already receiving more attention from researchers and practitioners, and are likely to have increased coverage in the media as well.

Finally, a particularly intriguing concept that will hopefully receive more attention is what Rothe and Friedrichs identify as 'crimes of globalization'.[11] The phrase refers to demonstrably harmful policies and practices of institutions and entities that are specifically a product of the forces of globalisation and that occur in a global context. These may include violations of statutory law, but they also include harms wherein the priorities of institutions and entities favouring the interests of the powerful and privileged result in harm to vulnerable people.

8.3.2. Women in Transnational Crime

An appropriate criticism of the increased attention on transnational crime is that it has a gender bias – both in terms of offenders and victims. That broad point is made very well by Barberet and needs no expansion here.[12] However, she does raise a point about women offenders that is relevant for any ruminating about future developments. Specifically, Barberet notes that world attention focuses more on women as victims than as offenders. When

---

[10] Thomas Barker, *Biker Gangs and Transnational Organized Crime*, Elsevier, Boston, 2015; Thomas Barker, *North American Criminal Gangs: Mexico, United States, and Canada*, Carolina Academic Press, Durham, 2015.

[11] Dawn Rothe and David Friedrichs, *Crimes of Globalization*, Routledge, New York, 2015.

[12] Rosemary Barberet, *Women, Crime and Criminal Justice: A Global Enquiry*, Routledge, New York, 2014.

there is scholarly interest on women offenders, it tends to be in (and about) Anglo-American cultures (Australia, Canada, the United Kingdom, and the US). Importantly, what we know about women offenders in developed Western countries cannot always be applied to the non-Western developing world. That is beginning to change as researchers look at the varied roles women play in transnational crimes in, for example, Africa.[13] Hopefully, the special issue devoted to women and transnational crime, in the journal 'Trends in Organized Crime' foretells increased attention to women in transnational crime.[14]

8.3.3. Civil Society and Private Business

One of the more interesting developments anticipated by several scholars in this field is the belief that entities other than national governments will play an increasingly important role in preventing and combating global crime. Transnational organisations such as the United Nations will play key roles for decades to come, as will more criminal justice-specific organisations such as Interpol and Europol. But there is also likely to be more involvement by the private sphere and by civil society. The role of governments and supra-national organisations is not expected to diminish, but we are likely to see an increased role for non-governmental organisations ('NGOs'), non-profit groups, and private companies (for example, ships increasingly use private security forces as they travel through areas at high risk for sea piracy).

Using the specific example of human trafficking, we see the involvement of supra-national organisations such as the United Nations' Global Initiative to Fight Human Trafficking, national-level government agencies like the US State Department's Office to Monitor and Combat Trafficking in Persons, major NGOs similar to the Organization for Security and Cooperation in Europe that are working to combat human trafficking, and private foundations such at the International Cocoa Initiative that works with

---

[13] Jana Arsovska and Popy Begum, "From West Africa to the Balkans: Exploring Women's Roles in Transnational Organized Crime", in *Trends in Organized Crime*, 2014, vol. 17, no. 1, pp. 89–109; Annette Hübschle, "Of Bogus Hunters, Queenpins and Mules: The Varied Roles of Women in Transnational Organized Crime in Southern Africa", in *Trends in Organized Crime*, 2014, vol. 17, no. 1, pp. 31–51; Marina Mancuso, "Not All Madams have a Central Role: Analysis of a Nigerian Sex Trafficking Network", in *Trends in Organized Crime*, 2014, vol. 17, no. 1, pp. 66–88.

[14] Arsovska and Begum, 2014, *ibid.*

labour unions and the chocolate industry to eliminating child labour and forced labour in cocoa farming and chocolate production. There is every reason to believe that this involvement of government, civil society, and the private sphere will expand, complement, and enrich the global response to transnational crime.

8.4. Conclusion

The goals of this contribution were to provide some insight into the current global legal environment regarding international and transnational crime, and to identify the direction that is likely to be taken in terms of global efforts in response to those crimes. Global efforts regarding international crime seem firmly placed in the formal sphere – and particularly with the ICC. There are important concerns regarding possible bias by the ICC, its pace, and the expense of its operation, but there is no reason to believe that it will cease functioning. Instead, the ICC will likely undergo reforms in terms of having clearer and more realistic goals.

Steps toward reform related to international crime broadly and the ICC more specifically, should occur on at least two fronts. First, issues raised regarding bias against African countries must be attended to and resolved. Of the 124 countries that have ratified the Rome Statute of the ICC, nearly one-third are African States. In 2016, three African countries (namely Burundi, the Gambia, and South Africa) announced their intention to withdraw from the ICC and other African Union countries have threatened to do the same. Discontent with the ICC from those countries (and others) include the above-mentioned perception of bias with prosecution seemingly focused on Africans; but there are also complaints of the ICC being a neo-colonial or paternalistic institution and one promoting Western interests. These are serious concerns that threaten the ICC's legitimacy – and even its existence. Rather than withdrawal from the ICC, resolution should involve collaborative leadership wherein African countries especially are actively and fully involved in efforts to review and refine ICC policy and procedure.

The second area for action should be the inclusion of terrorism as a crime over which the ICC has authority. The Rome Statute identifies genocide, crimes against humanity, and war crimes as falling within ICC jurisdiction to prosecute. It also allows the ICC to hear crimes of aggression, with jurisdiction over this category being activated in July 2018. Defining terrorism as a crime of aggression would provide the ICC with a broadened authority and give the Court additional credibility as an important twenty-first century institution. Clearly, this will not be easily accomplished given the absence of agreement on what constitutes terrorism. The ICC is an independent judicial institution, but the United Nations was key to its establishment. The United Nations should take the lead in having terrorism included within the ICC jurisdiction.

Global efforts regarding transnational crime are easier to identify and can be more clearly viewed as successful – but certainly not without need for improvement or expansion. Co-operation among nations is key in the response to transnational crime, and that co-operation must be extended and improved as the amount and types of transnational crime expands. There are several organisations particularly well-suited and well-positioned to take a leadership role in this area. The United Nations, especially the UN Office on Drugs and Crime, must continue and expand its efforts in such areas as development of model legislation on transnational crimes and various toolkits to be used by local law enforcement and NGOs. A UN initiative with particular promise is the 2030 Agenda for Sustainable Development, which includes a set of 17 Sustainable Development Goals to end poverty, fight inequality and injustice, and tackle climate change by 2030. Goal 16 is dedicated to the promotion of peaceful and inclusive societies that provide access to justice for all and build effective and accountable institutions at all levels. Specific action items in Goal 16 include reducing all forms of violence, combatting all forms of organised crime, reducing corruption and bribery, and using international co-operation to build capacity for combatting terrorism and crime. By using this goal, government and NGO efforts can be focused on specific steps for collaboration and action.

Other important areas for consideration include greater attention to the role of women in transnational crime, and the need for increased participation by civil society and private business. For example, our understanding of crime should be expanded to include social harm more broadly. In that way, scholars, practitioners, and policy-makers can give much needed attention to such topics as crimes against women in wartime, crimes against the elderly, and violence against children. The importance of such situations as extreme poverty, structural violence, and behaviours of desperation (survival sex, for example) in the context of transnational crime need the attention of researchers and action by civil society and policy-makers.

Hopefully, the result of such action will be a better understanding of, and appreciation for, the different ways that governments, organisations, institutions, and businesses can engage in global governance.

9

The Future of International Criminal Law:
A Practitioner's Perspective

Serge Brammertz and Kevin Hughes*

9.1. Introduction

International criminal law ('ICL') is facing an uncertain future. It is at the end of its beginning, but there are concerns that it may also be at the beginning of its end. Historic achievements have been made that even two decades ago would have been unimaginable. Yet these successes have bred more overt resistance, while it has become clear that ideals are often more difficult to realise in practice than initially understood. Understandably, attention is often focused on disagreements within the international community over the absence of criminal accountability for ongoing mass atrocities, such as with Syria. However, while it is important to continue expanding the space of accountability globally, the future of ICL will be as much determined by whether it is successfully implemented, particularly at the national level.

In this respect, it should be acknowledged that the results achieved to-date have not always been sufficient. The expectations of many for what ICL can achieve are often too high, but that is only a partial explanation. Manageable challenges remain unaddressed because past lessons are not heeded by professionals and policy-makers alike. Far too often common-sense solutions fail to receive necessary political and bureaucratic support, while at the same time well-meaning supporters are sometimes unwilling to acknowledge flaws that threaten the effectiveness and sustainability of the project.

---

* **Serge Brammertz** is Chief Prosecutor of the Mechanism for International Criminal Tribunals and the former Chief Prosecutor of the International Criminal Tribunal for the Former Yugoslavia. **Kevin Hughes** is Legal Advisor to the Prosecutor of the Mechanism for International Criminal Tribunals. The views expressed herein are those of the authors alone and do not necessarily reflect the views of the Mechanism for International Criminal Tribunals or the United Nations in general.

Fortunately, the volatility and rapid changes in the landscape of ICL over its short history are positive signs that the field is maturing. Experiences suggest that some challenges today should be seen as cyclical or inevitable in the formation of new norms. These challenges must be managed, of course, but they do not undermine the rationale for ICL in the long-term. More pressing at the moment may be challenges that cast doubt on whether ICL is in fact effective at re-achieving peace, security and stability in societies afflicted by conflict and the collapse of social order. It is no longer sufficient to rely solely on principles and ideals in advocating for accountability; the burden is now on ICL to show that it works.

Strategically, then, the focus for professionals, policy-makers and institutions in the near-term should be on improving the practice of ICL and thereby securing its foundations. Two decades of experience have shown key areas for attention in this regard that can be addressed. If managed correctly, the result will be a more mature field that has the necessary structures, tools and experiences to achieve results when called upon, and is well-prepared to continue promoting the spread of accountability in the future.

9.2. Overview

International criminal law concerns the prosecution of those responsible for so-called 'core international crimes': war crimes, crimes against humanity and genocide. While ICL violations can occur in a range of circumstances, in practice, the field to-date has primarily addressed post-conflict and transitional societies in which violations have occurred on a widespread and/or systematic scale. For this reason, prosecutions of ICL violations are correctly seen as part of broader transitional and international criminal justice endeavours.

Criminal accountability for massive violations of international humanitarian law is understood to help achieve important local and global goals. Most concretely, prosecutions serve to prevent and deter future violations. Punishment constrains the capacities of past offenders to re-offend – a key local outcome in transitional contexts – while also signalling to potential offenders that there will be serious consequences for future violations. More broadly, criminal accountability is correctly understood as essential to security and stability, which in turn are indispensable conditions to reconstruction and development. Peace and justice, historically

understood as alternatives, are thus now framed as complementary and mutually-reinforcing processes in constructing stable orders, both nationally and globally. Finally, and most ambitiously, the enforcement of ICL is often hoped to further the development of political order based on the rule of law, democratic and accountable government and respect for human rights. Nationally, ICL contributes to the domestication of international standards of criminal justice and respect for human rights. Globally, effective ICL is seen as an important component of an international order that is rules-based, liberal and equitable.

The speed and depth of ICL's development over the past two decades is evident. It was only in 1993 that the first modern international criminal tribunal – the International Criminal Tribunal for the Former Yugoslavia ('ICTY') – was established by the United Nations ('UN') Security Council. Since that time, international or internationalised tribunals to prosecute ICL violations have been established for Rwanda, Sierra Leone, Chad, Bosnia and Herzegovina, Kosovo, Timor Leste and Cambodia. To put this in context, no international criminal tribunals were established for almost fifty years after the post-World War II prosecutions at Nuremberg and Tokyo, a period that included devastating conflicts in, *inter alia*, Indonesia, Nigeria, Bangladesh, and Angola. Yet, nine tribunals have been created in just the last 23 years. This trend continues today, as proposals to establish new tribunals for contemporary conflicts are proliferating, including for South Sudan, Sri Lanka, and the Central African Republic, among others.

For many, these rapid developments culminated with the establishment of the International Criminal Court ('ICC') as the permanent, treaty-based international tribunal for core international crimes. The adoption in 1998 of the Rome Statute of the ICC was an enormous achievement, and a surprise in many respects. Efforts to create a permanent international criminal court had struggled since the UN General Assembly in 1948 first invited the International Law Commission to study the matter. Even until the last moment, it was not clear whether efforts to breakthrough deadlocks would succeed, and in the end the Rome Statute was adopted by vote over the strong objections of key states, including the United States and China as two of the five permanent members of the UN Security Council. With the 60th ratification in April 2002, the Rome Statute entered into force and the ICC was formally established. As of the date of writing, there are 123

States Parties, while a further 31 states have signed but not yet ratified the Rome Statute.

Over these last two decades, international criminal justice has shown that it can achieve important results in practice. Hundreds of individuals have been tried and convicted for war crimes, crimes against humanity and genocide, including 80 by the ICTY to-date and 62 by the International Criminal Tribunal for Rwanda. Those brought to trial include senior political leaders like Charles Taylor (President of Liberia), Jean Kambanda (Prime Minister of Rwanda), Hissène Habré (President of Chad), Nikola Šainović (Deputy Prime Minister of Yugoslavia), Radovan Karadžić (President of the *Republika Srpska*) and Nuon Chea (Prime Minister of Cambodia). Numerous senior military and paramilitary leaders have also been brought to trial, such as General Ratko Mladić (Commander of the *Republika Srpska* Army), General Dragoljub Ojdanić (Chief of Staff of the Yugoslav Army), Issa Sesay (leader of the Sierra Leonean Revolutionary United Front), Colonel Théoneste Bagosora (Chief of Cabinet in the Rwandan Ministry of Defence) and many others. Criminal prosecutions have also been brought against non-governmental actors, including religious, business and cultural figures. It is not an exaggeration to say that millions of victims in places like the former Yugoslavia, Rwanda, Cambodia and Sierra Leone have received some measure of justice for the crimes committed against them.

This strong record of successful prosecutions has had other benefits. Investigations and prosecutions have greatly contributed to the impartial establishment of historical facts. Independent judiciaries have confirmed that genocide was committed in Rwanda in 1994 and in Srebrenica in 1995. Cases have detailed the organised and systematic manner in which crimes were committed in Cambodia during the Khmer Rouge regime and by both rebel and pro-government forces in Sierra Leone's civil war. These are just a few of the many examples of how criminal prosecutions uncover the truth of what happened. While the facts of mass atrocities will always be contested in post-conflict societies, international criminal justice is uniquely positioned to offer an unbiased perspective that can be the foundation for agreement by societies on their shared past.

International criminal tribunals have also greatly contributed to the development of ICL. For example, while the 1948 Genocide Convention created the framework for the law of genocide, international tribunals have

answered many questions about how that law applies in practice. Contrary to popular understanding, genocide is not a question of how many people were killed. Rather, as international tribunals have consistently held, what distinguishes genocide from other crimes is the intent to destroy a group in whole or in part, and the jurisprudence that has developed offers critical tools to aid in this assessment. Similarly, international tribunals have greatly developed the law of command responsibility, which provides that political and military leaders can be held responsible for failing to prevent or punish the crimes of their subordinates in particular circumstances. This principle is of decisive importance; research has conclusively shown that the most effective way to prevent international crimes is by influencing the behaviour of organisational leaders.

One of the more notable recent developments in ICL has been the increasing attention paid to supporting accountability in national courts, which is typically described as 'complementarity'. Particularly in conjunction with prosecutions at the international level, national justice for international crimes has the potential to realise a wide-range of gains. Local justice is closer to the affected societies and thus may have more impact. It can also help to further reduce impunity, given the limited capacities of international tribunals alone to prosecute all those responsible for the crimes committed. For example, while the ICTY focused its prosecutions on nearly a hundred of the most senior leaders responsible for crimes, national courts in the former Yugoslavia are helping to ensure fuller accountability by prosecuting thousands of other mid- and low-level perpetrators. Finally, national justice is an opportunity for broader rule of law reform and expanding access to justice at the national level. By incorporating international standards and best practices and modelling effective criminal justice, national prosecutions of international crimes can be an important change mechanism for domestic justice sectors.

Yet even with the positive results that have been achieved in practice, there are valid impressions that international criminal justice can and should have achieved more, particularly in light of the financial and political investments that have been made. Perhaps most visibly, the impact of ICL in the former Yugoslavia is decidedly mixed. There have been two decades of peace, and there is general acknowledgement that crimes were committed by all sides to the conflicts. Yet while the most virulent forms of ethnic nationalism have largely retreated to the margins, the fact is that reconciliation has not been significantly advanced, and relations between societies remain dominated by historical grievances and mistrust. Ethnonational politics continue to be the rule, while ethnic insults and threats are still all too common in the public sphere. The region's troubled state was confirmed in 2015 when the UN Security Council failed to adopt a resolution commemorating the 20th anniversary of the Srebrenica genocide.

Similarly limited positive signs can be seen in other areas. In a number of situations, conflicts have persisted or newly-erupted even after criminal accountability processes began. In 2004 the Democratic Republic of Congo ('DRC') was among the first situations investigated by the ICC, yet the Kivu conflicts and M23 rebellion broke out subsequently, displacing hundreds of thousands more civilians and resulting in more widespread sexual violence and killings. Similarly, in the Central African Republic ('CAR'), a second civil war broke out in 2012, five years after the ICC opened investigations into crimes committed in 2002 and 2003. Marked by religious cleansing and possible signs of genocide, the current conflict in the CAR has displaced up to 900,000 civilians.

In these and other countries, accountability has been limited even once underway, creating the unfortunate appearance of token justice. Very few if any prosecutions have been completed to-date against perpetrators from any side for crimes committed in Uganda and Kenya at either the international or national level, notwithstanding that both situations are before the ICC and that both countries created specialized prosecution units for international crimes. For the DRC and the CAR combined, only five individuals have been brought to trial before the ICC so far, while none have for crimes committed in Libya and Sudan.

The absence of more successful results in situations where accountability mechanisms have been active can ultimately call into question whether international criminal justice is effective in practice. Of course, there are limits to what criminal justice can achieve on its own, and expectations are often too great. There will be external risks and challenges that greatly impact accountability initiatives but which are outside their control. Nonetheless, the fact remains that in a world of austerity and contests within the international community, political and financial resources are limited, and priorities have to be set based on the results that can be achieved. The practice of international criminal justice can and should be improved to ensure that the necessary support continues to be provided.

Thankfully, experiences offer many valuable lessons learned, three of which are highlighted below. Professionals, policy-makers and institutions now have the opportunity to improve international criminal justice and make it more effective for the future.

9.3. State Co-operation

All justice processes for international crimes over the last two decades have had to face the critical challenge of obtaining state co-operation. This dimension fundamentally distinguishes international justice from its domestic counterpart. In stable domestic orders, police and judiciaries expect and receive full co-operation from government and private actors. In transitional and post-conflict societies, such norms will have broken down, if they ever existed. International tribunals, which are wholly external to domestic structures and lack effective enforcement powers, can expect even greater difficulties in securing co-operation from state institutions and actors. The diverse experiences of justice institutions in overcoming these challenges highlight a number of key lessons for policy-makers, diplomats and professionals.

First, the willingness of affected states to co-operate with justice mechanisms must be seen as decisive to the success of accountability processes and a key factor to influence. In other words, international justice requires diplomatic influence and persuasion to succeed; it is not an alternative when persuasion has failed. While it may be hoped that international tribunals can achieve justice over the resistance of states, experience has shown this to be a high-risk strategy that is unlikely to deliver expected results. On the positive side, however, experience has also shown that state willingness to co-operate will be dynamic over time and can be engendered through co-ordinated diplomatic strategies aimed at influencing the behaviour of relevant states. As a consequence, policy-makers and institutions supporting accountability should see the commencement of justice processes as the beginning of their engagement, not the end. Referring a situation to the ICC or concluding an agreement to establish a hybrid tribunal are important first steps that then need to be followed by sustained diplomatic and political support.

The ICTY's experience with Serbia vividly demonstrates this lesson. For many years, ICTY fugitives lived openly in Serbia, secure in the knowledge that the Serbian government refused to co-operate with the

ICTY and arrest them. The Serbian government also withheld key evidence that was important to establishing the criminal responsibility of senior leaders. Yet sustained diplomatic engagement by the European Union and its member states, the United States and other key actors persuaded Serbia over time to improve its co-operation with the ICTY, ultimately leading to evidence being handed over and wanted fugitives being arrested. In these supportive states, justice in the former Yugoslavia was perceived as a national interest and enjoyed domestic political support. As a result, these states were able to successfully implement a linkage policy that conditioned financial assistance to Serbia and its European Union integration on Serbia's co-operation with the ICTY. While specifics will vary in each particular situation, this example shows the positive impact that co-ordinated diplomatic support and engagement can have on changing state behaviour with respect to accountability processes. Critically, it is important to realise that even if comprehensive justice is not immediately achievable, this does not mean that it is impossible to attain eventually.

Second, strategic pragmatism is often a necessary tool in pursuing accountability. Comprehensive justice must remain the ultimate goal. But because what is achievable will vary over time, an incremental approach may often be required, making sequencing a key factor. This is true with respect to both the co-operation of affected states and the diplomatic policies of supportive states, the latter of which is not always appreciated. Justice is only one among a number of potentially competing diplomatic priorities. While maintaining independence and impartiality, international justice must take this reality into account, not ignore it. At the same time, policy-makers and institutions should clearly signal their priorities and the diplomatic support they will provide. Contrary to what may be believed, the greatest risk to international justice is not when peace is the short-term policy priority for the international community, but rather when justice actors mistakenly pursue a dogmatic strategy that depends on diplomatic support it is not likely to receive. Such situations only lead to division, recriminations and the appearance of ineffective justice.

Third, affected states are more likely to agree to co-operate with justice mechanisms when the full spectrum of diplomatic tools is engaged and justice is linked to other desirable outcomes. This is strikingly evident from the former Yugoslavia. While financial assistance was a key component of conditionality policies, the attractiveness of the European model was an equally if not more powerful factor. Further, because international justice was directly linked to the justice chapter of the European Union *acquis*, public diplomacy was able to make clear that co-operation with international tribunals was not simply a condition for accession negotiations, but intrinsically linked to the legal, political and social structures responsible for European prosperity and stability.

9.4. National Participation

Another key lesson has shifted the paradigm for international justice: it is now clear that meaningful accountability cannot be achieved without the participation of national courts. Even the most successful international tribunals can only prosecute a limited number of cases against those most responsible for crimes. The ICC is likely to be even more constrained. As the ICTY's experience has shown, fuller accountability requires co-operation with national courts. If initially it was believed that international tribunals would be the default forum for prosecuting international crimes, the reality is in fact the opposite: accountability projects should begin with national courts and incorporate international mechanisms when necessary. This lesson has a range of important policy implications.

First, it is necessary to re-appraise how the essential elements of international justice can be best delivered, and careful attention should be given to innovative solutions that have proved their value in practice. This would begin by recognising that the international community's primary interest is in the fair and effective prosecution of international crimes, not the particular mechanism through which that is achieved. Given the importance of supporting the rule of law in post-conflict and transitional societies, it becomes clear that national justice offers greater potential to achieve more benefits and synergies than international tribunals. From this perspective, the task is to support national accountability for international crimes by ensuring that it is fair and enabling it to be effective.

A number of tools have been developed to help achieve these goals. Hybrid tribunals such as the Special Court for Sierra Leone have proved effective, while organisations like the Organization for Security and Co-operation in Europe have developed experience in monitoring war crimes trials in national courts. Practitioners have also repeatedly identified embedded international advisers as a valuable tool that has been underutilized to-date. One of the most successful experiments has been the War Crimes

Chamber in the State Court of Bosnia and Herzegovina. By temporarily integrating international judges and lawyers into a national court, this project was able to create a strong national foundation for further prosecutions of international crimes. There were significant results in building the capacity of the local judiciary, and the participation of internationals improved public trust in the fairness and impartiality of the process.

Second, there are still only rudimentary processes and structures in place for international assistance to national judiciaries in post-conflict and transitional societies. For example, UN peacekeeping and special political missions are increasingly mandated to support the rule of law, resulting in the establishment, *inter alia*, of UN Police. But, while in 2012 more than 14,000 police officers were deployed across 16 UN missions, there were only 315 judicial affairs officers who were limited to advisory roles. Similarly, very few if any national governments or international organisations have established capacities and procedures to provide human resources to support national judiciaries, which would include not only lawyers and judges, but also forensic specialists. While the creation of organisations like Justice Rapid Response is a step in the right direction, much more remains to be done.

Finally, the nationalisation of international justice must also involve courts in third-party states. Experience has repeatedly demonstrated that conflicts and massive human rights violations create significant population flows to third party states, a reality being seen again today with the Syrian conflict. Refugees will include victims, witnesses and perpetrators of international crimes, so even in countries far removed from the conflict, accountability for international crimes will become a domestic justice issue. Addressing the challenge of cross-border international crimes requires national prosecutors in the affected and third-party states to work together collaboratively. Building the capacities of courts in the affected countries will benefit domestic judiciaries, and vice versa.

9.5. Integration

The development of ICL has been contemporaneous with a significant increase in international attention to peace-keeping, peace building and post-conflict reconstruction. These latter fields have undergone important reforms in the last twenty years, among the most important of which has been the increasing integration and co-ordination of activities into more coherent country-wide programmes, seen, for example, in the establishment of the UN Peacebuilding Commission in 2005 and the trend to multi-dimensional peace-keeping operations and special political missions. However, today the integration of international criminal justice with broader peace building and reconstruction efforts is still largely at the early stages.

It is critical to recognise that rule of law activities in general cannot be separated from accountability for international crimes, as has sometimes been the tendency. Because of their notoriety and impact, prosecutions for international crimes will greatly influence public perceptions of the rule of law and justice sector in post-conflict and transitional societies. Moreover, international criminal justice offers a unique opportunity to catalyse civil society and members of the public in support of rule of law reform, while also providing a model for effective and impartial justice that can then be applied in other legal sectors. Better outcomes can be achieved in the future by ensuring a coherent approach to rule of law issues in post-conflict and transitional societies that fully integrates and benefits from international justice initiatives also underway.

Likewise, there are many opportunities in other sectors to make better use of criminal justice processes for international crimes. Prosecutions will generate valuable evidence and intelligence that can assist a wide range of peace building activities, from identifying potential hotspots of renewed conflict to compiling lists of victims for medical and mental health treatment. For example, investigations conducted by the ICTY in Bosnia and Herzegovina greatly contributed to vetting police officers suspected of participating in crimes, which was essential to building trust in police organisations. Crime mapping exercises can also help establish immediate priorities for humanitarian assistance and rebuilding efforts.

9.6. Conclusion

Policy-makers and institutions addressing ICL issues are faced with an uncertain environment. With strong diplomatic and public support, the field has expanded dramatically in recent years and become an integral part of discussions on what is needed in post-conflict and transitional societies. Many real achievements have been secured, and it is now clear that accountability for international crimes, including at the highest political and military levels, is possible. For many states, support to international criminal justice is now a key foreign policy priority.

Yet, at the same time, the way forward from here can seem unclear. Resistance to accountability is becoming stronger and more overt, and repeated attempts to establish justice processes for the most serious current conflicts have failed. Concurrently, the initiatives that have been created have not always achieved the full results that were expected. In some situations, circumstances appear little changed even after a decade of work, and other more recent initiatives seem to be following the same trend line.

What has been proposed here is that in the near-term, the strategic focus should be on improving the practice of international criminal justice by reflecting on experiences and lessons learned from the first two decades of work. The risk of ineffective justice is both critical and manageable. This is not to minimise the importance of structural and geo-political issues, but rather to suggest that a focus on implementation at the moment offers the opportunity to achieve important results that will better position the field in the long-term. Key lessons that have been specifically identified include securing state co-operation, nationalising international justice and integrating accountability into broader peace building and reconstruction efforts. Building on these and other lessons learned will help confirm that accountability is not only right in principle, but also effective in practice at rebuilding order and ensuring sustainable peace.

10

The Global Climate Constitution

René Lefeber*

10.1. Introduction

The adoption of the 2015 Paris Agreement under the United Nations Framework Convention on Climate Change ('Paris Agreement') has been hailed and revered by key players in climate governance as "a climate revolution" and "the beginning of the end of the fossil fuel era".[1] Others have been more cautious and have described the Paris Agreement as "an important step in the evolution of climate governance and a reaffirmation of environmental multilateralism".[2] Yet such reaffirmation is not devoid of significance after the failure of the 15th Climate Change Summit in Copenhagen in 2009 to produce a legally binding agreement and the rejection of the 1997 Kyoto Protocol to the United Nations Framework Convention on Climate Change ('Kyoto Protocol') as the legal framework for combating climate change.[3]

In 1997, the adoption of the Kyoto Protocol had been hailed and revered as "the unprecedented, legally enforced ambition of limiting and reducing the greenhouse gas emissions that have accompanied the rise and rise of the industrial era".[4] It contained a modest objective, namely a reduction of overall emissions of greenhouse gases by at least five percent by industrialized countries below 1990 levels in the first commitment period

---

* **René Lefeber** is Professor of International Environmental Law at University of Amsterdam.

[1] See International Institute for Sustainable Development, "A Brief Analysis of the Paris Climate Change Conference", in *Earth Negotiations Bulletin*, 2015, vol. 12, no. 663.

[2] *Ibid.*

[3] The US never became a party and even unsigned the Kyoto Protocol; Canada withdrew from the Protocol; and Japan, Russia and New Zealand have not accepted commitments under the Protocol beyond 2012.

[4] See International Institute for Sustainable Development, "A Brief Analysis of COP-3", in *Earth Negotiations Bulletin*, vol 12, no. 76.

from 2008 to 2012. Although this objective has been achieved,[5] by the end of 2014, global emissions had increased by 60% since 1990.[6]

The objective of the Paris Agreement is to hold "the increase in the global average temperature to well below 2°C above pre-industrial levels and to pursue efforts to limit the temperature increase to 1.5°C above pre-industrial levels".[7] Achieving this objective requires deep reductions in global emissions of greenhouse gases, more precisely to no more than 40 gigatons annually. The Climate Change Summit in Paris recognised that the intended actions will not suffice to keep the increase in the global average temperature to below 2°C above pre-industrial levels.[8] The projected level of emissions in 2030 is 55 gigatons and, hence, the projected emissions gap in 2030 is 15 gigatons. The Paris Agreement is a first step, as was the Kyoto Protocol in 1997, as was the United Framework Convention on Climate Change ('Convention' or 'UNFCCC') in 1992.

The Convention provides the legal framework for both the Kyoto Protocol and the Paris Agreement. The ultimate objective of the Convention is the stabilisation of the concentrations of greenhouse gases in the atmosphere at a level that would prevent dangerous anthropogenic interference with the climate system.[9] The Convention does not, however, provide for a holistic approach to protect the atmosphere, because it does not address other forms of atmospheric pollution, such as the depletion of the ozone layer or long-range transboundary air pollution. It only provides for the governance of climate change.

10.2. Responding to Climate Change

Since the adoption of the Convention, mitigation and adaptation are the cornerstones of the international community's efforts to achieve the

---

[5] See Secretariat of the United Nations Framework Convention on Climate Change, Annual Compilation and Accounting Report for Annex B Parties under the Kyoto Protocol, UN Doc. FCCC/KP/CMP/2016/6.

[6] Global Carbon Project, *Global Carbon Budget 2015*, Future Earth and International Geosphere-Biosphere Programme, 2015, slide 7.

[7] Paris Agreement, 2015, Article 2.1(a).

[8] United Nations Framework Convention on Climate Change, Report of the Conference of the Parties on its Twenty-First Session, Held in Paris from 30 November to 13 December 2015, Decision 1/CP.21, UN Doc. FCCC/CP/2015/10/Add.1, para. 17.

[9] United Nations Framework Convention on Climate Change, 1992, Article 2.

Convention's objective. Mitigation of climate change seeks to control global warming through the regulation of the concentrations of greenhouse gases in the atmosphere that have an anthropogenic origin. These concentrations are a function of the emissions of greenhouse gases by 'sources' and their removals by 'sinks'. Both emissions and removals may have either an anthropogenic origin or a natural origin. Sources of an anthropogenic origin are, for example, the burning of fossil fuels, while an example of a source of a natural origin is volcanic eruption. An example of a sink of an anthropogenic origin is the capture and storage of greenhouse gases, and an example of a sink of a natural origin their absorption by oceans and vegetation. Energy efficiency and saving, the use of sustainable energy sources, and comparable human efforts contribute to the mitigation of climate change.

Adaptation to climate change presupposes that a certain degree of global warming is inevitable and that the international community must prepare itself for the resulting global changes in physical and biological systems, including a sea level rise and land degradation. Adaptation is the adjustment of physical or human systems, in connection with a real or expected change of the climate and its consequences, with the aim of reducing the vulnerability of those systems to climate change. In case of sea level rise, adaptation could be achieved through the maintenance of natural barriers, such as dunes and mangrove forests, the creation of buffer areas for water, the construction and reinforcement of sea barriers and, if such measures are not effective or no longer cost-effective, the abandonment of land.

According to the Intergovernmental Panel on Climate Change ('IPCC'), neither mitigation nor adaptation alone can avoid all climate change impacts.[10] The IPCC had already found in 2007 that mitigation and adaptation can complement each other and together can significantly reduce the risks of climate change. The assumption was that the international community will come to a timely agreement on effective arrangements for mitigation and adaptation, that all members of the international community will commit themselves to these arrangements, and that each member of the international community will comply with them. The agreement was

---

[10] Rajendra K. Pachauri and Andy Reisinger, *Fourth Assessment Report, Climate Change 2007: Synthesis Report*, Intergovernmental Panel on Climate Change, 2007, p. 65.

adopted in 2015, but it remains to be seen whether the agreement is timely and effective, all member of the international community will express their consent to be bound by it, and each party will comply with it.

The acceptance by the international community of an increase in the global average temperature above pre-industrial levels means, however, the acceptance of injurious consequences as a result of global warming. The implementation of mitigation and adaptation measures could result in a significant reduction of the risks of climate change, but not in their elimination. In spite of the implementation of mitigation and adaptation measures, the international community will have to face the injurious consequences of climate change. The magnitude of these consequences will also depend on the effective implementation of new mitigation and adaptation measures. It is expected that the Earth will be confronted more frequently with increasingly serious natural disasters and slow onset events, including flooding as a result of heavier storms and sea level rise. It is possible to be better prepared for these disasters through the development and improvement of contingency plans, disaster relief plans, temporary shelter arrangements for displaced persons, and compensation mechanisms for victims. In addition to mitigation and adaptation, 'acceptance' of those injurious consequences (in the form of loss and damage) has become a new component of climate change policy. At the 19th Climate Change Summit, the Warsaw International Mechanism for Loss and Damage Associated with Climate Change Impacts was adopted,[11] and actions to address such loss and damage are envisaged in Article 8 of the Paris Agreement.

The international community has not, at least not yet, resorted to 'climate engineering' to combat climate change. 'Climate engineering' is the deliberate large-scale manipulation of the planetary environment to counteract anthropogenic climate change. Such manipulation may take the form of the removal of greenhouse gases from the atmosphere (carbon-dioxide removal) or the management of the radiation of the sun (solar-radiation management). The anthropogenic removal of greenhouse gases from the atmosphere reduces the concentrations of these gases in the atmosphere and, hence, contributes to mitigation of climate change. Solar-radiation

---

[11]   United Nations Framework Convention on Climate Change, Report of the Conference of the Parties on its Nineteenth Session, Held in Warsaw from 11 to 23 November 2013, Decision 2/CP.19, UN Doc. FCCC/CP/2013/10/Add.1.

management seeks to enhance the capacity of the Earth to deflect sunlight (by blocking sunlight before it reaches the surface of the Earth) or reflect sunlight (by enhancing the capacity of the Earth's surface or clouds to reflect sunlight). Solar-radiation management does not change the concentration of greenhouse gases in the atmosphere and, hence, does not contribute to mitigation of climate change. The international community has never seriously addressed climate engineering at the Climate Change Summits, but the same international community has adopted a non-binding moratorium on climate engineering that may affect biological diversity under the Convention on Biological Diversity (except for small scale scientific research studies in a controlled setting).[12]

10.3. The Old Global Climate Constitution

At the first Climate Change Summit in Berlin in 1994, the international community recognised that the adoption of the Convention was a first step in combating climate change and that additional steps would be required to prevent dangerous anthropogenic interference with the climate. The Summit agreed to a process, known as the Berlin Mandate, that culminated in the adoption of the Kyoto Protocol in 1997. Following the elaboration of additional measures clarifying its implementation modalities, the Kyoto Protocol entered into force in 2005. The first commitment period under the Protocol ran from 2008 to 2012. The 18th Climate Change Summit in Doha in 2012 adopted an amendment to the Kyoto Protocol establishing the second commitment period from 2013 to 2020. The Kyoto Protocol provides for:

- successive binding individual economy-wide emissions targets for industrialized countries;
- a market-based approach through the establishment of international emissions trading mechanisms enabling industrialized states to achieve emissions targets at marginal costs;
- a robust accounting system to measure, report and review the emissions of industrialized countries; and

---

[12] Convention on Biological Diversity, COP 10 Decision X/33, para. 8(w). Specific methods of climate engineering have been addressed under other international agreements, such as ocean fertilization under the 1996 Protocol to the 1972 Convention on the Prevention of Marine Pollution by Dumping of Wastes and Other Matter.

- a self-enforcing mechanism to secure industrialized countries' compliance with their binding commitments by making these countries either comply with or withdraw from the Kyoto Protocol.[13]

The Convention, together with the Kyoto Protocol, constitutes the Old Global Climate Constitution. This Old Constitution is characterised by:

- a focus on the mitigation of emissions from industrialized countries with minimal attention for adaptation and no attention for acceptance;
- internationally agreed and enforceable commitments to achieve environmental integrity and avoid free riding;
- recognition of the historic responsibility of industrialized countries for human-induced climate change through a strict application of the principle of common but differentiated responsibilities and respective capabilities with respect to emissions targets; and
- resort to free market mechanisms to facilitate emissions reductions.

10.4. The New Global Climate Constitution

At the 21st Climate Change Summit in Paris in 2015, the international community adopted a new global climate constitution, consisting of the Convention and the Paris Agreement. Following the failure of the 15th Climate Change Summit in Copenhagen in 2009, the international community demonstrated the continued viability of multilateralism through the adoption a legally-binding agreement attached to a decision complementing the agreement with clarifications and additional actions pending its entry into force. On 4 November 2016, the Paris Agreement entered into force. It provides for:

- successive nationally determined contributions of all countries, which they intend to achieve, to mitigate climate change;
- the establishment of a mechanism enabling the international transfer of national mitigation outcomes;
- the enhancement of adaptive capacity, strengthening resilience and reducing vulnerability to climate change;

---

[13] Canada withdrew from the Protocol in 2011 after it had become clear that it would not be able to meet its emissions target in time.

- the recognition of the importance of averting, minimising and addressing loss and damage associated with the adverse effects of climate change with the understanding that this does not involve or provide a basis for any liability or compensation;
- binding commitments for developed countries to provide financial resources, technology and capacity-building to assist developing countries with their mitigation and adaptation commitments;
- a flexible transparency framework to share, technically review and multilaterally consider information from all countries on the implementation of their mitigation and adaptation commitments;
- a regular assessment of collective progress towards achieving mitigation and adaptation as well as the means of implementation and support ('global stocktake'); and
- a mechanism to facilitate and promote compliance of all countries with their respective commitments.

The New Global Climate Constitution is characterised by:

- enhanced action on adaptation to build climate resilience and attention for acceptance to address the injurious consequence of climate change, because global warming can no longer be avoided and mitigation alone no longer suffices to address climate change;
- unilaterally determined mitigation efforts with the aim of setting all countries on an irreversible trajectory to a balance between anthropogenic emissions by sources and removals by sinks of greenhouse gases in the second half of this century (climate neutrality);
- a perpetual cycle of determining, sharing, reviewing and considering mitigation and adaptation commitments which has been designed to avoid the need to resort to amendments to scale up efforts to combat climate change;
- the continued recognition of the principle of common but differentiated responsibilities and respective capabilities by permitting developing countries to move over time to emissions reduction or limitation targets and requiring developed countries to provide financial resources, technology and capacity-building to assist developing countries with respect to their mitigation and adaptation commitments; and

- less reliance on market-based mechanisms as a result of the change in the legally binding nature of the mitigation commitments.

The New Global Climate Constitution is more inclusive in terms of participation in the efforts to mitigate climate change and, therefore, potentially more effective in achieving the objective of the Convention. Although the unilateral nature of the mitigation efforts increases the risk of free riders, it would appear that that has become less of a concern, as mitigation is no longer only associated with costs, but also with economic opportunities.

There has been a regime change, but the old and new regimes will co-exist, at least for the time being. Although the second commitment period under the Kyoto Protocol covers less than 15 percent of global emissions, the international community has not agreed to discard the old regime. The adoption of the Paris Agreement is nevertheless a paradigm shift in the global effort to combat climate change. The Kyoto Protocol is expected to wither, even if the Doha Amendment enters into force, giving the second commitment period a sound legal basis.

10.5. Regime Change Drivers

Climate change is a threat to human survival on Earth. At the beginning of the twenty-first century, the Old Global Climate Constitution was no longer universally endorsed. The United States – at the time the country with the largest share of global emissions – refused to participate in it, giving as one of its main reasons that developing countries were not required to contribute to the reduction of global emissions. The deadlock could only be overcome after science demonstrated that the dangerous anthropogenic interference with the climate system could only be avoided if all countries would contribute to mitigation.

The mitigation efforts of only two countries, China and the United States, that were responsible for 27 percent and 15 percent respectively of global emissions in 2014,[14] could make a difference, but the costs of mitigation do not induce unilateral action. Although an effective response to climate change is not possible without mitigation efforts of these countries, they cannot dictate the efforts of other countries either. Hence, a multilateralist approach is required if all countries are to be involved in the response

---

[14] Global Carbon Project, 2015, see *supra* note 6, slide 9.

to climate change. A multilateralist approach based on consensus, which is the default for decision-making under the Convention, requires sufficient time to understand and accommodate respective interests, and is likely to result in the lowest common denominator. Yet it produces a result that stands the best chance to secure the legitimacy and effectiveness of a constitutional framework addressing a global threat.

Scientific findings, as developed by the IPCC, demonstrated that the dangerous anthropogenic interference with the climate could only be avoided if all countries would contribute to mitigation. These findings enabled diplomats, with the assistance of governmental experts, to negotiate and adopt the New Global Climate Constitution. It provides the indispensable point of reference for the further development of climate law at all levels of governance (national, supranational, international and transnational).

The Paris Climate Change Summit has welcomed the efforts of stakeholders and invited them to scale up their efforts to combat climate change.[15] This appeal is addressed, amongst others, to the private sector that is responsible for emissions. Although it had already been pointed out in 1997 that "[t]he private sector is also the key target group for the political signals from Kyoto that business as usual is no longer an option",[16] the introduction of market-based approaches (in the form of carbon trading) proved to be susceptible to fraud and may not have resulted in the reduction of emissions as intended. The New Global Climate Constitution may have created the momentum for the emerging public-private partnerships and private-sector initiatives that contribute to mitigation, adaptation and acceptance of climate change, including the mobilisation of financial resources. It may become the point of reference for an action agenda that could include policies and measures by:

- regulatory authorities that ban fossil fuel activity beyond the Antarctic (see Article 7 of the Antarctic Treaty Protocol on Environmental Protection) to other vulnerable regions, such as the Arctic high seas;

---

[15] United Nations Framework Convention on Climate Change, Decision 1/CP.21, see *supra* note 8, paras. 134–135.

[16] See International Institute for Sustainable Development, "A Brief Analysis of COP-3", *supra* note 4.

- tax authorities that create a level-playing field on the energy market to ensure the internalisation of environmental costs of energy production, that is, the elimination of fossil fuel subsidies and the introduction of carbon pricing, including accompanying trade measures;
- territorial authorities, including cities and regions, that are directed towards building a resilient infrastructure and sustainable transportation, for example, smart grids and electric public transport;
- insurance companies to reduce their vulnerability to an increased exposure to weather risks, not by adjusting contractual restriction and raising premiums, but by encouraging their clients to implement cost-effective risk-reducing adaptation measures;
- investment funds to move away from investments in fossil fuels towards investments in renewable energy;
- Individuals to change our contemporary life styles, for example, by insulating our homes, our holiday destination closer to home, and enjoying more vegetarian meals; and
- civil society to put the implementation of the New Global Climate Constitution on the agenda, not only by calling for actions such as those above at all governance levels, but also by playing a role in its enforcement.

Since the beginning of this century, there has been a proliferation of climate change related cases in courts around the world. Many of these cases have been initiated by civil society. Claims have been submitted for the relief of procedural injury, such as the failure to take into account climate effects in environmental impact assessments; injunctory relief for the failure of governments to take adequate mitigation or adaptation measures; or compensation for loss and damage resulting from climate change. Such public interest litigation has not been without success. Courts have sometimes resorted to creative legal engineering to hold defendants to account for their lack of action to combat climate change. Public interest litigation may also be directed to promoting or enforcing compliance with mitigation commitments under the New Global Climate Constitution. In particular, it may prevent regression of successive nationally determined contributions. Although the effort-oriented nature of a nationally determined contribution makes it legally difficult to enforce it in a court of law, such contribution may be enforceable in a court of law once achieved and succeeded by a new nationally determined contribution.

The increasingly complex global society enables and requires a holistic legal approach with initiatives at all levels of governance to combat global problems that threaten human survival. The Global Climate Constitution provides the legal basis for and leaves room for legal actions at other governance levels to complement it and give effect to it. The regime change has cost valuable time, there is not much more time to lose.

INDEX

TOAEP TEAM

OTHER VOLUMES IN THE
LAW OF THE FUTURE SERIES

Sam Muller, Stavros Zouridis, Morly Frishman and Laura Kistemaker (editors):
The Law of the Future and the Future of Law: Volume II
Torkel Opsahl Academic EPublisher
The Hague, 2012
Law of the Future Series No. 1 (2012)
ISBN: 978-82-93081-80-7

Sam Muller and Stavros Zouridis (editors):
Law and Justice: A Strategy Perspective
Torkel Opsahl Academic EPublisher
The Hague, 2012
FICHL Publication Series No. 2 (2012)
ISBN: 978-82-93081-82-1

Ayelet Berman, Sanderijn Duquet, Joost Pauwelyn, Ramses A. Wessel and Jan Wouters (editors):
Informational International Lawmaking: Case Studies
Torkel Opsahl Academic EPublisher
The Hague, 2012
FICHL Publication Series No. 3 (2012)
ISBN: 978-82-93081-84-5

All volumes are freely available online at http://www.toaep.org/lotfs/. For printed copies, see http://toaep.org/about/distribution/. For reviews of earlier books in this Series in academic journals and yearbooks, see http://toaep.org/reviews/.